Cambridge Elements ≡

Elements in American Politics
edited by
Frances Lee
University of Maryland

ROLL CALL REBELS

Strategic Dissent in the United States and United Kingdom

Justin H. Kirkland
University of Virginia

Jonathan B. Slapin
University of Essex

CAMBRIDGE
UNIVERSITY PRESS

University Printing House, Cambridge CB2 8BS, United Kingdom

One Liberty Plaza, 20th Floor, New York, NY 10006, USA

477 Williamstown Road, Port Melbourne, VIC 3207, Australia

314–321, 3rd Floor, Plot 3, Splendor Forum, Jasola District Centre, New Delhi – 110025, India

79 Anson Road, #06–04/06, Singapore 079906

Cambridge University Press is part of the University of Cambridge.

It furthers the University's mission by disseminating knowledge in the pursuit of education, learning, and research at the highest international levels of excellence.

www.cambridge.org
Information on this title: www.cambridge.org/9781108701556
DOI: 10.1017/9781108568883

First published 2019

A catalogue record for this publication is available from the British Library.

ISBN 978-1-108-70155-6 Paperback
ISBN 9781108628044 Online
ISSN 2515-1592 print
ISSN 2515-1606 online

Roll Call Rebels

Strategic Dissent in the United States and United Kingdom

Elements in American Politics

DOI: 10.1017/9781108568883
First published online: January 2019

Justin H. Kirkland
University of Virginia

Jonathan B. Slapin
University of Essex

Abstract: Scholars of legislative politics often note the many differences between the British House of Commons and the US House of Representatives. These include differences in party strength, members' partisan loyalty on votes, and general institutional structure. Because of these differences, scholars have rarely compared these chambers directly. This Element aims to do precisely that. The authors point out the many similar motivations of members in both chambers, and leverage these similar motivations to theorize that member ideology and party agendas interact to produce party disloyalty. Using data on legislative voting following changes in agenda control, the authors demonstrate that ideological extremists in both the United States and United Kingdom use party disloyalty to connect with ideologically extreme constituents. The similarities in patterns across these chambers suggest that legislative scholars have much to gain by considering the commonalities across American and British politics, and in general, by thinking more frequently about US legislative politics in a comparative context.

Keywords: legislative politics, House of Representatives, House of Commons, party loyalty, ideology

ISBNs: 9781108701556 (PB), 9781108628044 (OC)
ISSNs: 2515-1606 (online), 2515-1592 (print)

Contents

1 Introduction

The United States and the United Kingdom, two of the oldest representative democracies in the world, share a long, intertwined history. The countries are culturally and politically similar with shared norms around the importance of the rule of law, a commitment to basic political rights, and a belief in free markets. One thing that they do not share, though, is a political system, at least with respect to institutions. Across the range of democratic institutions in the world today, the United States and the United Kingdom are very different, and researchers often place them on opposite ends of the spectrum. The US system is both presidential and federal, while the United Kingdom is parliamentary and unitary. Classic works on comparative political institutions discuss the United States as possessing features of "consensual democracy" and contrast it with the majoritarian, Westminster system of the United Kingdom (Lijphart 1999); or they discuss the United States as having many veto players compared with the United Kingdom's single veto player (Tsebelis 2002). UK parties are thought of as highly disciplined (Spirling and McLean 2006; Dewan and Spirling 2011) while US parties remain relatively weak, even when compared to other presidential democracies (Carey 2009). And the list could go on.

Yet other seminal works on democratic representation suggest that the incentives for politicians to engage with their voters, often through constituency service, to cultivate a "personal vote" are not so different (Cain, Ferejohn, and Fiorina 1987). Both countries have a two-party system and, for the most part, use first-past-the-post majoritarian electoral systems where ballots (and election campaign materials) prominently feature individual candidates, often over the parties they represent. In short, politicians in both countries seek to build personal connections with their electorates.

While scholars of democracy at least since de Tocqueville (1966) have been making comparisons between the United Kingdom and United States, very few have explicitly compared legislative behavior – the nature of activities that elected members engage in while serving in the legislature. Indeed, the large differences between American presidential and British parliamentary democracy might lead us to believe that such a comparison could bear very little fruit. Studies of voting behavior in the UK House of Commons usually note just how different the Commons is from the US Congress (Kam 2009; Spirling and McLean 2006). Recent works on party discipline in legislatures have focused on Westminster systems (Kam 2009), parliamentary systems (Proksch and Slapin 2015), or presidential systems (Carey 2009), with few making comparisons across these systems.

But if we accept that electoral systems – and the incentives that they create – affect how voters view politicians and how politicians seek votes, and if we accept that politicians (at least occasionally) attempt to represent constituents' views on the floor of the legislature, then we might expect to find some similarities in how members behave between the United States and the United Kingdom despite their many institutional differences. These similarities may, at times, be difficult to tease out as they are buried among the weeds of the political, institutional, and cultural differences that persist between the two political systems. Nevertheless, we believe that through new theorizing about the relationship between voters and politicians, we can identify similar patterns in these legislatures that teach us something new about democracy and representation in both countries.

We argue that members of the legislature – the House of Commons in the United Kingdom and Congress in the United States[1] – have similar incentives to develop a "personal" vote, that is, to develop a persona, independent from the party, to connect with constituents and win votes; and they often do so by dissenting from their party's stated position on the floor of the legislature. As political scientists have long known, aggregate patterns of dissent look quite different in these two systems; ideological moderates tend to rebel to occasionally support the opposing party in the United States, while ideological extremists are more rebellious in the United Kingdom. In this short Element, we develop a theory that helps us uncover instances of similarity. We demonstrate that ideology and majority party agenda control interact to affect the likelihood that members rebel against the majority position within their party in both countries. More precisely, members who are most ideologically extreme vote against the majority of their party with relatively greater frequency when their party controls the legislative agenda. We argue that they do so because their party's control of the legislative agenda provides them with opportunities to connect with ideologically motivated constituencies, either their own geographical constituents or ideologically demanding interests within their party.

1.1 Case Selection

As scholars of the American and British politics, we want to know what the politics of each country can tell us about politics in the other. And as scholars of comparative institutions, parties, and elections, we are interested in how the electoral motivations of parties and their candidates for office shape members' legislative activity once elected – namely, the electoral connection. Because we wish to focus on the impact of this electoral connection in two-party first-past-

---

[1] Our theory applies to both the US House and Senate, but empirically we focus on the House.

the-post systems, the United States and the United Kingdom are natural cases to turn to. Recent literature on case selection, comparative methods, and mixed methods research has suggested that the best way to engage in "controlled comparison" is to demonstrate that a general theory holds across different cases that vary in meaningful ways. It argues for using large-N empirical analysis within a single case to offer evidence of the internal validity of a causal theory, and small-N empirical work across cases to explore external validity (Slater and Ziblatt 2013). We engage in case-specific quantitative work to demonstrate that our theory works in two different, but related settings.

The United Kingdom and the United States provide the optimal test cases for our theory. On a macro level, they have relatively similar political cultures including a shared legal tradition, long histories with electoral politics, and democratic norms that have evolved over centuries. They are wealthy, industrialized nations with Anglo-Saxon market economies (Hall and Soskice 2001) and possess similar welfare regimes (Esping-Andersen 1990). Party politics in both largely conforms to competition on a single left-right ideological dimension between two main parties. In both countries, a right-wing party favors social conservativism, low taxes, and lower government spending while a left-wing party represents social liberalism and more government intervention in the economy. Moreover, American and British politicians draw inspiration from each other, as when Tony Blair sought to emulate Bill Clinton in creating a "third way" for center-left politicians, and more recently (and perhaps more bizarrely) when Nigel Farage, former leader of the UK Independence Party, campaigned with Donald Trump during his 2016 presidential campaign. In comparing the United States and United Kingdom, we can make a reasonable claim to hold constant many socio-economic and macro-political variables.

However, the political institutions of US and UK politics are quite different. Over the course of the long nineteenth century, the United Kingdom developed into a parliamentary democracy, with the government serving with the confidence of Parliament, strong and unified parties, and government agenda control (Cox 1987). Parliament and its committee system are quite weak in terms of lawmaking abilities (Mattson and Strom 1995). Although there has been devolution of powers to Scotland, Wales, and Northern Ireland, the political system remains highly centralized with ultimate authority resting in Westminster, typically under a single-party government. We can juxtapose the UK system with the US system – both federal and presidential – which vests legislative authority in the bicameral Congress, has relatively weak parties, and gives the executive significantly less power to control the legislative agenda. The relative weakness of American parties has led scholars to even question the value of accounting for parties in models of legislative behavior at all (Krehbiel 1998). And in contrast to the House of Commons, the US Congress is marked by powerful committees and a strong seniority norm (Shepsle and Weingast 1987; Krehbiel, Shepsle, and Weingast 1987).

American and British democracy quite simply rest on different institutional models of democratic politics – except for the fact that they use single-member districts in which candidates from two main parties compete against one another for the seat. Through careful within-case analysis we offer evidence for our model.

1.2 Our Theory: An Overview

Both British and American electoral politics revolve around personal connections between candidates and voters. During campaigns, election materials prominently feature candidates' images and names. Candidates engage in constituency service, answer constituents' requests, and spend significant time in their constituency. But once we move out of the district and back to Washington and Westminster,[2] the similarities are assumed to end. Generally speaking, American members of Congress see their behavior as an extension of their own electoral campaigns (Mayhew 1974). Partisan control in Congress is relatively weak, and partisan dissent within Congress is quite common. Members view dissent as potentially electorally beneficial, and the spatial model suggests that these rebels ought to come from the ideological center (Kirkland 2014).

Research on UK legislative politics also suggests that voting against one's party can be electorally beneficial to individual MPs (Campbell et al. 2016; Vivyan and Wagner 2012). But parties are often unified, and Westminster politics is highly partisan. There are fewer opportunities to rebel on votes (divisions in British parlance), and doing so is generally costlier than it would be in the United States. Moreover, instead of coming from the center of the political space, rebels tend to come from the ideological extremes of the party (Benedetto and Hix 2007).

Given that the electoral systems of both countries encourage members to engage in behavior that helps them to distinguish themselves from their party, we seek to uncover ways in which rebelliousness in the United Kingdom and United States is similar despite the significant differences in partisan control that result from the nature of presidential and parliamentary democracy.

---

[2] The difference in American and British terminology is worth noting here. The British speak of constituencies, and the Americans refer to districts. We use the country-specific terminology when writing about each country separately, but when making comparisons between the two we often use terminology interchangeably.

Extant research on party rebellion (especially in the US context) offers a relatively simplistic view of when and why representatives defect from their party's position on a vote. Based mostly on proximity models of ideological voting, existing theories suggest that legislators compare the policies produced by a bill under consideration to the policies that would result if the bill failed to pass. Additionally, depending on the sophistication of the model, legislators take into account any wrath representatives incur from party leaders for their defections and any possible rewards from voters. Most of these models (but not all) predict that defections primarily come from ideologically moderate members of opposition parties. Moderates hold ideological positions closer to the other party and governing (or majority) parties have more carrots to entice moderates to cross the aisle. While some of these patterns hold up to empirical scrutiny, others are on less-solid footing.

We offer a new theoretical explanation for party disloyalty during legislative voting. It differs from the existing literature in two ways. First, our theory provides a new account of the role of legislative agenda-setting in leading members to defect from their party, and second, it takes voters' response to defections more clearly into account. In our model of defection, legislators use disloyalty to signal ideological purity to voters when their party is in the majority (or government), but not when in the minority (or opposition). Ideologically extreme legislators from the majority (governing) party can generally expect their party's policies to pass. With this knowledge, they can take ideological positions through rebellion. They can vote against their party to draw attention to themselves and to argue that their leadership should use its time in office to pursue a more ideologically "pure" agenda. They do so while knowing that policy is likely moving in their preferred direction and their rebellion is unlikely to affect outcomes. We call this behavior "grandstanding," which we define as signaling an ideological position to voters through rebellion or opposition, even to policies that the legislator might otherwise prefer, without directly affecting policy.

Our expectations emerge from the simple notion that ideologically extreme constituents expect ideologically committed behavior from their representatives. We argue that members of the party with agenda control can differentiate themselves from the rest of the party through rebellion. They can sell an ideological message to a particular set of ideologically motivated constituents without looking as if they support the policy programs of the opposing party. Members of the party that lacks agenda control are unable to defect without appearing to lend support to the policy program of the competing party.

Over the next two sections, we illustrate our model with several examples from British Parliament and the US Congress, and lay out the general expectations from our model, which apply to any legislative system that uses single-member electoral districts to select its members.

1.3 Data, Evidence, and Empirical Strategy

The evidence we provide is observational. We use publicly available data from legislative repositories to show how individual MPs change their behavior over time as legislative agenda control shifts. In effect, we examine within-individual changes in behavior as party control of the agenda (winning or losing a legislative majority) shifts – change in agenda control becomes our "treatment" variable.[3] We examine how individual MPs, and ideologically extreme individuals in particular, change their rebellious behavior as agenda control shifts. It is only recently that such a research design has become feasible, both for reasons of data availability, but even more importantly due to the course of history.

In the United States, Democrats controlled a majority in the US House of Representatives for 40 years from the 84th Congress in 1955 through the 103rd Congress, ending in 1995. Since then, control shifted to the Republicans during the Gingrich revolution in 1995, returned to the Democrats for two terms from 2007 to 2011, shifted back to Republicans in 2011 with the new Tea Party faction gaining seats, and returned to Democratic control in 2019. From 1955 until 1995, members could have had very long careers in Congress, having only ever served in the majority or the minority. To find members who have served in both, we would either need to return to the era of Roosevelt, Truman, and Eisenhower, or look at the recent era from the 1990s to the present.

Likewise, for the period for which we have access to good data, British governments (and parliamentary majorities) have tended to be quite long lasting, meaning we as scholars need to wait quite a long time to view alterations in power. The Tories under Margaret Thatcher and then John Major were in power for eighteen years from 1979 until 1997. Labour under Tony Blair and Gordon Brown held power for thirteen years from 1997 until 2010. And today, the Conservatives have held power under David Cameron and Theresa May since 2010, albeit in coalition with the Liberal Democrats between 2010 and 2015. It is only recently that history has provided us with enough alterations in power to say something meaningful about agenda control and rebellion.

1.4 Plan for the Element

We begin in the next section by offering a detailed look at the politics of our two cases, and we make a case for comparing them with respect to legislative

---

[3] Note that we cannot offer a true difference-in-difference design as all members of the same party are subject to shifts in agenda control at the same time.

behavior. Section 3 then presents our theoretical argument. Combining aspects of spatial proximity models and behavioral theories of voter evaluations of representatives, we develop novel expectations about how ideology, agenda control, and electoral circumstance motivate party rebellion.[4] Whereas comparative legislative scholars often learn about politics by applying models developed in the US context to other systems, here we demonstrate that we can also learn about US politics by thinking about US legislative behavior in terms of models usually reserved for studying the politics of Westminster.

In the fourth section, we present our primary empirical evidence by examining voting behavior of the British House of Commons and the US House of Representatives. We test our theory using model specifications that explicitly explore the interactive effects of ideology and legislative agenda control (governing status) to predict rebellions. We demonstrate that while in the aggregate legislative behavior looks very different in the two countries, on the margins, ideological extremists behave similarly. They are relatively more loyal when their parties are in opposition (the minority) and less loyal when in government (the majority). We then go on to examine various configurations of divided government in the United States and demonstrate that the United States looks most similar to the United Kingdom when Congress and the President are controlled by different parties. We suspect that under divided government the majority party in Congress moderates its stance to pass bills acceptable to the President, opening up ideological space for rebellion on the party's wings.

In our concluding section, we briefly reflect on the institutional differences and behavioral similarities of our two cases, and we discuss how we imagine partisan legislative politics evolving within each nation moving forward. We also discuss how our model and findings might apply to other cases beyond the United States and the United Kingdom.

2 Why the United States and United Kingdom?

We start this section with a few questions: Why compare the politics of the United States and United Kingdom? Why focus on legislative behavior? And why do so now? We start with the last question first as the answer (at least to us) seems obvious, and we will provide answers to the other two before the end of the section.

---

[4] One more note regarding terminology: whereas American Congress scholars often reserve the term "rebellion" for significant unrest within the party often aimed at overthrowing the Speaker of the House or some other large-scale insurrection, British politics scholars often use the term to refer to voting against the party. Perhaps the difference arises because votes against the party are rarer and more significant in Britain. We use the terms "rebellion" and "dissent" interchangeably to refer to one or more members voting against the majority of the party in the legislature.

It would be an understatement to say that the last few years have seen significant political upheaval in both the United States and the United Kingdom. In many ways, the changes on either side of the Atlantic mirror each other. And despite the vast differences in political systems, they have made the two countries look more similar. In addition to making these cases substantively interesting to examine, we believe that some of these changes can been viewed as a consequence of the type of behavior that our model seeks to explain – ideological appeals to voters by legislators on the fringes of their party. In the final section, we re-examine these changes in light of our model and evidence.

Within the last 15 years, arguably the main parties in both countries have lost control of leadership contests for the party's highest office holder. The politics of both countries have seen waves of populism, culminating in the "Brexit" vote to leave the European Union and its aftermath in the United Kingdom, and the election of Donald Trump in the United States. But we have also seen a recent trend towards youth engagement in politics, especially during the UK 2017 election, and also in support of Bernie Sanders in 2016 in the United States. Relatedly, the main parties have seen local activists asserting power and shaping candidate selection contests in ways that have had profound effects on politics at the national levels. In both countries, these changes have led to growing fissures within the main parties. Given these changes, comparing the politics of these two countries is even more important now than ever before. We can take the opportunity to gain new insights about American politics by looking at the politics of the United States's closest ally, and new insights about Britain by peering across the pond at Americans. Far too little work in political science has made these comparisons explicitly, but rarely has there been a better time to do so.

2.1 Political Change in the United Kingdom

Anthony King, the eminent scholar of British politics, recently wrote that the nature of the British political system has changed significantly since the initial postwar period of 1945–1970 (King 2015). During the postwar period, as King eloquently describes in the opening chapter of his book, the party controlling a majority in Parliament ruled the roost; parliamentary parties were highly disciplined, in control of their leadership contests, and power was clearly centralized in Westminster. He argues that by 2015 – the time of the book's publication – much about British politics had changed. With the advent of the Brexit vote to leave the European Union and the recent Labour leadership contests, it has arguably changed even more in the interim. For our purposes, the changes that matter most are those that have increased the role of voters in the political process and, in particular, have increased the role of ideologically driven local party activists, often the audience for MPs' rebellious dissent.[5]

King describes how MPs have ceded control over party leadership contests, and thus over who leads the party into the next election, becoming Prime Minister should the party win. In the past, the Conservative Party's sitting MPs chose the leader of the party. On the Labour side, the leader was voted on by a tripartite electoral college of sitting MPs (and Members of the European Parliament), party members, and trade unions, each group having equal weight when voting; but the MPs put forward the candidates (each requiring the support of 12.5 percent of sitting MPs and MEPs). However, these rules have changed. Tory MPs still decide on the top two candidates for party leader, but these two candidates are put to the rank-and-file membership for a vote. In 2001, the rank-and-file chose Ian Duncan Smith as party leader even though a substantial majority of Conservative MPs preferred Kenneth Clarke, who also polled better in the general electorate.

Arguably, Labour MPs have done even worse in retaining control of the leadership selection process. The parliamentary Labour Party has always fought battles with left-wing local activists who have played a large role in selecting (and less frequently, de-selecting) MPs (Tsebelis 1990; King 2015). However, with the possible exception of the leadership of Michael Foot (1980–83), the parliamentary party has always managed to maintain control of the upper echelons of the party. In the three most recent leadership contests, though, the first choice of the parliamentary Labour Party was not elected leader. And in both the 2015 and 2016 contests, their least favored candidate, Jeremy Corbyn, came out on top. Labour Party rules have long meant that the parliamentary Labour Party could be outvoted by the membership and labor unions. In 2010, Ed Miliband became Labour Party leader with strong union-backed support despite the fact that the parliamentary party and the Labour membership preferred his brother David Miliband, who also was polling better among the public. Not only did this lead to an epic rift in the Miliband family, but it led Labour to change its rules for leadership elections.

With the 2015 leadership contest, the party did away with the electoral college, instead deciding to hold all future leadership contests on the basis of "one member, one vote." The idea behind the rules change was that union members would have to opt-in as affiliate members rather than have a vote by default. The parliamentary Labour Party only retained the ability to put forward candidates,

---

[5] There have been other significant changes as well, such as reforms to the House of Lords under Tony Blair's government and the introduction of the Fixed-Term Parliament Act, to name just two.

albeit with a slightly increased hurdle for support among the parliamentary party – signatures from 15 percent of MPs plus MEPs. Simultaneously, the party created a new category of membership – registered supporters – which allowed people to vote in the leadership election after paying a mere £3.

After the 2015 general election, Ed Miliband stepped down as leader following his loss. Some in the parliamentary party felt that it would be good for the slate of candidates to have more ideological diversity. So along with party frontbenchers and supposed frontrunners Andy Burnham, Yvette Cooper, and Liz Kendall, long-time rebel and general thorn-in-the-side-of-the-party Jeremy Corbyn found his way onto the ballot. Corbyn was not taken seriously by party insiders, who hoped that his nomination might quiet some on the left. Instead, Corbyn proved to be the resounding favorite of the Labour Party membership, winning the leadership in 2015 and then retaining it in a second contest in 2016.

But these changes are minor compared to the political earthquake that was the Brexit vote. Of course, the decision itself was decided by referendum – an unusual event in British politics. The only two previous nationwide referendums were the failed 2011 vote on introducing an alternative vote electoral system and the referendum on membership in the European Community in 1975. The 2016 referendum was the result of a split within the Tory Party that was precipitated by both anti-EU sentiment among activists within the Conservative Party and the rise of the UK Independence Party (UKIP) (UKIP) (Clarke, Goodwin, and Whitely 2017). Those who voted for the United Kingdom to leave the EU were largely older voters, concerned about immigration, feeling economically vulnerable, and worried about losing British sovereignty. In the aftermath of the vote, there was an uptick in violence against foreigners, especially those from Eastern Europe – in late summer 2016 three Polish citizens were murdered in Harlow, in one example. In short, David Cameron called the vote largely to try to silence vocal anti-EU activists in the party, who were flexing relatively new muscles, and to fend off UKIP, a new party. The outcome was marked by a rise in nationalism and populist sentiment – features that had played a much lesser role in British politics only a few years earlier.

Changes in the nature of leadership contests along with the Brexit vote represent actions and appeals to mollify the ideological wings of the Labour and Conservative parties, respectively. Such actions have become increasingly common in recent years.

2.2 Political Change in the United States

Recent changes in American politics mirror those in Britain. American parties have never been as strong or as centralized as British parties, nor have they ever enjoyed the ability to control the races for the top office in the same way that British parties (usually) can. Nevertheless, in most presidential contests, candidates supported by party elites have managed to come out on top. Even following the McGovern-Fraser reforms in the mid-1970s, which changed the nature of presidential primaries to allow for more voter participation, parties have managed to coalesce around a single candidate (Cohen et al. 2008). And prior to the McGovern-Fraser reforms, smoke-filled rooms had been the norm. In the last few elections, however, it is not so clear that parties got their way. In 2008, Hillary Clinton was the early favorite of Democrats, only to lose to Barack Obama. Then in 2016, the Trump bombshell hit the Republican Party. Largely thanks to a crowded nomination field, and institutional changes limiting the control of party elites over nominations, real estate mogul and television personality Donald Trump managed to take command of the Republican Party primary.

Many of these internal party changes mirror events within parties in the United Kingdom. The Republican Party changed their rules concerning "superdelegates," linking their votes to the primary contest candidate that their state voted for. The 2015 change provided more influence for rank-and-file voters, and less top-down control of nominations for party elites. This arguably more open nominating system prevented the party from rallying behind a more traditional, establishment-friendly candidate. Over the course of the nomination contest, Republican elites attempted to rally the party behind Jeb Bush, Marco Rubio, John Kasich, and several other experienced candidates, only to see their lack of control over the contest allow Trump to sweep away challengers. Within the Democratic Party, an insurgent left-wing offered persistent vocal support to Bernie Sanders, who had previously spent his entire career as an independent and only caucused with the Democrats, turning what party elites would have preferred as a virtually uncontested nomination into a heated debate about the ideological identity of the party itself.

These nomination contests suggest that both US parties have a large faction of voters interested in ideological purity who reject political compromise as a desirable attribute among leaders. While these factions likely do not represent a majority of either party (neither Sanders nor Trump secured a majority of voters in either nomination contest), they do represent a large, vocal portion of the parties with which politicians might gain favor by offering uncompromising rhetoric and behavior. Indeed, in the time since his election, the Trump-led Republicans have been through a variety of scandals that would otherwise deeply damage a party's collective reputation (including failures to condemn white supremacists and separating children from their parents at the US border), but like the UK voters in support of Brexit, Trump's core base remains loyal to his message.

Not only have US parties lost some control over candidate selection for their top posts – presidential candidates – they are simultaneously polarizing and becoming more ideologically distinct from one another. This had led to higher levels of party-line voting in Congress and, in the words of Thomas Mann and Norm Ornstein, has made US politics look more like politics in Westminster (Mann and Ornstein 2012). Arguably this polarization has been driven primarily by ideological right-wing groups within the Republican Party, starting in the era of Newt Gingrich and the "Republican Revolution" of 1994 when Republicans regained control of the House for the first time in 40 years (Theriault 2013). The rise of these groups has led to an increasing number of ideologically driven members of Congress willing to buck the party leadership – namely the Tea Party caucus within the Republican Party. These individuals, in particular, behave in a manner similar to ideologically extreme backbenchers in a Westminster system (Kirkland and Slapin 2017).

Thus, in both the United States and the United Kingdom, the major parties are experiencing ideological polarization and changing internal dynamics within their legislative parties. We see social cleavages among their electorates opening doors for more extreme national policies that would have been considered impossible in prior generations. Institutional changes, meanwhile, limit the control of party elites over nominations for top positions in government. These changes have led to both policy and institutional changes that experts in neither country were prepared for, and for which the ramifications are poorly understood.

2.3 The Value of Comparing UK and US Legislative Behavior

American and British politics have recently experienced similar political upheaval making our study timely. But what is the scientific value of comparing legislative behavior in these two countries, in particular? Studies rarely compare these countries directly, and certainly not with respect to legislative behavior. Cain, Ferejohn, and Fiorina (1987) provide one of the few examples. In their book, the authors examine the link between constituency service and the "personal vote" in both countries. However, the literature citing this book has focused largely either on American politics, for example looking at the link (or lack thereof) between the personal vote and incumbency advantage (King and Gelman 1991), or British politics and the puzzle of why, in a party-centric system, MPs spend time on personal vote-seeking at all (Norris 1997). Meanwhile, prominent studies in comparative politics cite the book as demonstrating the important role that electoral incentives can play in leading politicians to develop a personal vote, and therefore engage in constituency case work, even when they neither explicitly examine the United States nor the United Kingdom (Carey and Shugart 1995; Kitschelt 2000; Tsebelis 1995).

Institutional differences lead to stark contrasts in legislative behavior. In the United States, ideological moderates are more likely than extremists to cross the aisle to vote with the other party (Kirkland 2014), loyalty can be electorally costly (Carson et al. 2010), and as a result, parties (in comparative perspective) are simply not that disciplined (Carey 2009). In the United Kingdom, in contrast, ideological extremists are on average more likely to vote against their own party (Benedetto and Hix 2007; Dewan and Spirling 2011; Slapin et al. 2018) but party unity is high. While rebellion may help individual members on the margins, it can also hurt their parliamentary careers as parties value loyalty greatly (Kam 2009).

Nevertheless, these political systems share an electoral system that leads members of Congress and Parliament to create a personal vote and to seek a constituency connection, just as Cain, Ferejohn, and Fiorina (1987) described in their seminal book over thirty years ago. Both the United States and the United Kingdom use single-member districts with first-past-the-post elections to elect the members of their main legislative chambers.[6] Candidates' names appear prominently on the ballot, and the personas of the individual candidates feature heavily in electoral campaigns. Voters often know the name of their representative and they value the ability to make a personal connection with someone in politics.

Legislators elected from geographically defined, single-member district constituencies may wish to cultivate a set of supporters who vote for them not because of their affiliation to a political party, but because of their own personal attributes. Where electoral rules allow legislators to put their names on the ballot and campaign materials, they may wish to (and be able to) partially protect themselves from the misfortunes of their own party. In the United Kingdom, MPs may have good reason to worry about the effects of leaving the European Union on their parties' fortunes, and as such, would prefer if their electoral fates were not perfectly tied to that of their party. In the United States, members of Congress (MCs) face a similar calculus, whereby each individual

---

[6] There is some variation in electoral rules within both countries, especially for elections to different levels of government. The United Kingdom, for instance, uses a list PR system for electing members of the European Parliament, while regional elections to the Scottish and Northern Irish parliaments use mixed member proportional and single transferable vote systems, respectively. There is also variation within the US at the state and local levels. For investigations of the effects of this variation, see Bagashka and Clark (2016) and Rogowski (2017).

MC has incentives to protect him or herself from the harm that disagreements between Trump, establishment Republicans, and Democrats might do to their party brands. Thus, individual legislators have good reasons to attempt to "untie" their electoral fortunes from that of their parties as best they are able.

Members can generate a "personal vote" through activities they undertake within their districts. They attend the openings of public buildings and spaces, give speeches, attend parades and events, and hold office hours at their district offices. While clearly important to voters and politicians alike, these are not the activities that we focus on. Rather, we examine how members represent constituents and foster a political personality separate from the party through the activities they undertake in the legislature. We believe that legislative activity holds a special place in eyes of legislators and voters. Legislatures around the world often carve out specific times in the legislative calendar for members to engage in activities related to constituency representation.[7]

Voters value hearing MPs voice their concerns in a national forum with all of the pomp that comes with legislative debate. Two recent British examples make this point. First, shortly after Donald Trump was elected President, talk emerged that he would be invited to the United Kingdom for a state visit. However, shortly after taking office he announced a "Muslim Ban" barring citizens from seven Muslim-majority countries from entering the United States. The policy caused short-term chaos at the US border and immediately ran into trouble in the US court system. It temporarily affected British citizens who held dual citizenship in one of the affected countries. In the United Kingdom, Trump's policy was renounced across the board, with MPs lining up to criticize Trump and many suggesting that it would now be inappropriate to invite him for a state visit. MPs posted statements on websites and Facebook pages, they attended protests in their constituencies, but importantly they also set aside time for an official debate on the subject in Parliament.[8]

In another example, this one on the lighter side, an MP, Bernard Jenkin, representing areas surrounding the University of Essex[9], together with the Speaker of the House, John Bercow, an alumnus of the university and university chancellor,[10] organized an adjournment debate on the recent accomplishments of the university, which included moving up in the university league tables along with several other achievements. Adjournment debates take place

---

[7] In Ireland, question time tends to serve this purpose (Martin 2011), while in Chile the "incidents hour" (*Hora de Incidentes*) allows MPs to raise constituents' concerns on the floor (Alemán, Ramirez, and Slapin 2017).

[8] See https://hansard.parliament.uk/Commons/2017–01-30/debates/448738C3-927F-481B-8340-809810F30595/ChangesInUSImmigrationPolicy

[9] The employer of one the authors.

[10] A figurehead position at the top of the university organization.

at the end of the day usually on symbolic issues aimed at constituency issues or other non-controversial issues of importance to particular MPs. Students from the university, along with several faculty members and the university vice-chancellor,[11] attended the debate in the House of Commons, which received attention in university publications and news feeds.

These anecdotes (and especially the second) are examples of what Americans might call "mom and apple pie" debates (or votes). They are largely uncontroversial topics with symbolic value only.[12] No policy would change as a result of the floor activity. However, the debates do demonstrate that MPs value the ability to use floor time to express opinions they view as important to constituents. The MPs could have just as easily said everything they wanted to say in speeches in the constituency (and often they did that as well). But making their point with Parliament as a backdrop was clearly important to them.

Of course, of greater interest to us than these symbolic activities are those that result from a conflict between a member (or group of members) and the party. We wish to explore how members use floor activity to differentiate themselves from the rest of their party when acting on issues that are not purely symbolic (even if the members' behavior is largely symbolic). Legislators seek to communicate with their constituents about their activities and ideological positions (Grimmer 2013b), and they may specifically seek to use debates and votes to differentiate themselves from others in their party to the extent that they are able (Kam 2009; Proksch and Slapin 2015; Kirkland and Slapin 2017; Slapin et al. 2018). When core constituents adhere to a particular ideology or set of beliefs, they may value hearing their positions espoused on the floor of the legislature and legislators may connect with voters through ideological messages. Voters may value uncompromising behavior, and even rebellion, from those representatives (Campbell et al. 2016).

Members, though, are also constrained in their ability to dissent from their party. Although party loyalty is higher in the United Kingdom than in the United States, parties in both countries value unity. Dissension within parties may be damaging to a party's electoral brand (Kiewiet and McCubbins 1991; Cox and McCubbins 2005), and usually denotes a party struggling to enact its own policy program. Thus, the leadership of political parties in both the United States and United Kingdom have considerable incentives (and tools) to encourage loyalty among their party members (Pearson 2015; Kam 2009). Those same leaders,

---

[11] The British equivalent of a US university president.

[12] While Trump's "Muslim Ban" was almost uniformly denounced as bad policy, there was a disagreement over whether it meant that he should be denied the honor of a state visit. Many MPs pointed out that numerous dictators had been granted a state visit and that while the policy was distasteful, it was not a reason not to hold a state visit.

however, also value control of government. To control government, individual legislators must be allowed to pursue paths that help ensure their re-election, which may include some level of party disloyalty. Much like individual members who face competing incentives towards loyalty (not betraying their party) and disloyalty (appearing independent), party leaders have incentives to enforce unity (ensuring a clear party brand) and to allow dissension (potentially winning elections). Thus, there is reason to believe that, despite the significant institutional differences, the similar electoral systems may lead us to some similarities in patterns of legislative activity across both countries.

2.4 Summary

From our discussion in this section, we hope it is clear that while there are important institutional differences between the US and UK legislative systems, there are good reasons to think there exist key, previously unexplored, similarities. Moreover, the current political situation makes these similarities even more important to explore. Given the longstanding relationship between the two nations, the existence of similarities should not be terribly surprising. The US Congress was developed by members of colonial assemblies, who borrowed much institutionally from their experiences in the United Kingdom. Elections, efforts at representation, two-party politics, and personal votes are all important components of individual legislative strategy in both countries. These similarities, rooted in electoral politics, are likely to drive legislative behavior now perhaps more than ever, given increased levels of polarization in both countries. Changes in nomination rules across the major parties in both countries have also exacerbated many of these electoral motivations. That is, we agree with Norman Ornstein and Thomas Mann's assessment that the US Congress is becoming increasingly like a Westminster system, and we would go further to say that Westminster is slowly taking on some attributes of American legislative politics. These recent changes and motivational similarities ought to make our interest in comparing behavior across the countries all the more timely.

3 A Theory of Strategic Party Rebellion

Daniel Diermeier, writing about formal models of legislative politics, suggests that "research on legislatures has largely progressed along geographic divisions. The extensive literature on the US Congress has developed in isolation from the equally lively research on coalition government in parliamentary democracies" (Diermeier 2014, 45). Not only does Diermeier's statement ring true to us, but we believe that the literature on the British Parliament is perhaps even further removed from the theoretical debate. Models of the American Congress do not shed much light on Westminster parliamentary democracy, and the United Kingdom rarely experiences coalition government. Nevertheless, spatial models of politics have helped to shape our understanding of the US Congress, parliamentary politics, and British politics, albeit in different ways. In this section, we put forward a theoretical model to explain rebellion on the part of MPs in both the United States and the United Kingdom, helping to bridge the divide between the modelling of US congressional and British parliamentary behavior.

Our understanding of legislative voting is largely shaped by spatial proximity models (Downs 1957; Romer and Rosenthal 1978). In these models, actors cast a vote for the proposal that most closely represents their ideological views, often comparing any new proposal against the status quo policy (the current policy) or a reversion point (what would happen in the absence of change). Such spatial proximity models, coupled with models of legislative agenda control, provide the basis for many of our key theoretical insights into legislative behavior and organization, particularly in the United States (Denzau and Mackay 1983; Cox and McCubbins 1993, 2005; Krehbiel 1998; Shepsle and Weingast 1987; Krehbiel, Meirowitz, and Wiseman 2015) but also in parliamentary democracies (Huber 1996; Laver and Shepsle 1996; Tsebelis 2002). They inform us about the nature of policies that we expect to come up for a vote and which MPs ought to support these policies.

The proximity model of legislative decision-making has been highly successful in describing the roll call voting behavior of members of the US Congress (Poole and Rosenthal 1997), and it forms the basis for most of our tools used to estimate legislative ideal points (Poole and Rosenthal 1985; Clinton, Jackman, and Rivers 2004; Carroll et al. 2013). In comparative context, spatial models are used less to explain individual voting patterns (as recorded votes are rarer in many parliamentary systems) and more frequently as a tool to explain coalition formation and government breakdown (Laver and Shepsle 1996) or policy change (Tsebelis 2002). Meanwhile, the spatial model is ill-equipped to explain legislative voting in Westminster where party discipline is so high (Benedetto and Hix 2007; Spirling and McLean 2006). Rather, scholars of British politics tend to see the model as a foil against which to pit other theories of legislative behavior (Dewan and Spirling 2011; Kam 2009).

In this section, we present a theory that links spatial logic in roll call voting with a behavioral model of voter decision-making to explain rebellious voting behavior in both the United States and the United Kingdom. Before we present our model, though, we begin by motivating our theory with a few tales of legislative rebelliousness in the United States and the United Kingdom, followed by a description of literature with respect to American and British politics.

3.1 Tales of Rebellion

In Congress, spatial voting models suggest that party defectors should come from the ideological middle – moderate members of Congress may occasionally cross the aisle to vote with the other party (Poole 2005). Joe Manchin III, the Democratic Senator from West Virginia, offers a prime example of this type of party dissident. Since Donald Trump took office, Manchin has voted with the Trump administration more than any other Democrat.[13] Representing a rural, conservative state reliant on the mining industry, it is not surprising that he sides with Republicans on occasion. High party loyalty would likely cost him at election time. Being a member of the minority party, the Democrats do not have much to lose from him crossing the aisle. And if they prevented him from doing so, they might risk losing a valuable seat. In short, Manchin seems to represent spatial voting at work.

But not all members fit the "Manchin" pattern all of the time. During his time in Congress, Ohio Democrat Dennis Kucinich's (D-OH 10th) voting record placed him reliably among the most liberal members of Congress. Likewise, Texas Republican Ron Paul's (R-TX 14th) voting patterns were consistently among the most conservative. Both men attracted media attention for possessing an independent streak and for their failed presidential campaigns. While Kucinich and Paul may have held steadfastly true to their ideological roots, their partisanship on roll call votes varied significantly across time and followed a remarkably similar pattern. When their parties were in the minority they were highly loyal partisans; but once their parties secured a majority, they defected with greater frequency. Kucinich voted with the majority of Democrats on 96 to 97 percent of votes during the 108th, 109th, and 112th Congresses while in the minority. With the Democrats in the majority during the 110th and 111th Congresses, Kucinich's loyalty dropped to 93 percent and 91 percent respectively. When Republicans were the majority party prior to the 110th Congress, Paul voted with his party on between 70 percent and 78 percent of votes. When in the minority during 110th and 111th Congresses, his loyalty increased to 86 percent and 89 percent, respectively. With the Republicans once again holding the majority in the 112th Congress, his loyalty fell back to just over 80 percent.[14]

---

[13] According to www.fivethirtyeight.com as of September 10, 2018.

[14] The average majority party level of party loyalty across our sample is 87.23 percent.

Moving across the pond to the United Kingdom, we find that ideological extremists, and not moderates, are more likely to rebel (Benedetto and Hix 2007). During David Cameron's first term as Conservative Prime Minister, Philip Hollobone – a socially conservative member of the Tory right wing – was the most rebellious MP in the House of Commons. He voted against his own party leadership in 19.9 percent of votes, a remarkable figure in Westminster where party cohesion is typically very high. However, in the previous parliament when Labour was in government and his Tories were in the opposition, he rebelled against his own party leadership just 4.3 percent of the time. Nor is he alone. On the other side of the aisle, Jeremy Corbyn and John McDonnell were consistently two of the most rebellious Labour backbenchers, that is, prior to 2015 when they became Party Leader and Shadow Chancellor, respectively. However, both were much more rebellious when Labour was in government than when in opposition. During the 2005–2010 Labour government under Blair and Brown, Corbyn voted differently than the majority of his party a whopping 25.1 percent of the time, with McDonnell not far behind at 23.4 percent. However, while in opposition during the 2010–2015 parliaments, the two men only rebelled on roughly 5 percent of divisions.

In the aggregate, the behavior of ideological extremists in the United States and the United Kingdom appears different – the American ideologues much more loyal to their parties compared with moderates, and British moderates more much loyal than extremists. But on the margins, when looking at changes in rebellious voting as a function of agenda control, the patterns look much more alike. Just like Dennis Kucinich and Ron Paul, who were more loyal when their party was in the minority and more rebellious in the majority, Hollobone, Corbyn, and McDonnell were more loyal when their party was in opposition than in government. The shifts in the voting patterns of ideological extremists in Congress and Westminster look very similar, and it is this similarity that we seek to explain.

3.2 Rebellion and Party Discipline in the Literature

The patterns displayed by these ideological extremists are puzzling when considering the dominant models of legislative behavior, especially those meant to explain voting in Congress (Aldrich and Rohde 2001; Cox and McCubbins 1993; Krehbiel 1998). No current model of Congress suggests defection patterns should change depending on the partisan control of the House. In Westminster, where both theoretical and empirical models regularly account for very high levels of party unity, a government-versus-opposition divide, and extremist rebellion (Baughman 2004; Gaines and Garrett 1993;

Kam 2009; Spirling and Quinn 2010; Dewan and Spirling 2011), the link between agenda control, ideology, and rebellion has also not been fully explored.

Indeed, the proximity voting model has very little to say about parties and their involvement in legislative decision-making (Krehbiel 1998). It assumes that individual legislators cast roll call votes under no (or very weak) party constraints. This is, in fact, the reason why scaling models of roll call votes do not work well in the House of Commons or other parliamentary systems where partisan pressure and strategic voting are the norm (Spirling and McLean 2006; Bütikofer and Hug 2015). In the American literature, despite, or perhaps because of, the ubiquity of the proximity model, scholars have dedicated much effort to finding evidence for the role of parties in Congress (Aldrich 1995; Binder 1996, 1997; Cox and McCubbins 1993, 2005; Rohde 1991), and to assessing the conditions under which our empirical models can distinguish between situations of weak party and strong party governance (Krehbiel 2000; Krehbiel, Meirowitz, and Romer 2005; Clarke, Jenkins, and Monroe 2017). However, as Krehbiel (2000) notes, most measures of party influence on roll call votes examine aggregate party unity using Rice (Rice 1925) scores (e.g., Binder 1996) or support for party leadership votes (e.g., Cox and McCubbins 1993). Krehbiel (1993, 2000) demonstrates that these aggregate measures are particularly poor at distinguishing between situations of weak and strong party influence. None of these empirical studies in search of party influence look at individual legislators' decisions to defect from their party on votes.

Despite not saying much about parties, the spatial model does have important implications for party loyalty, some of which have been recently called into question (Dewan and Spirling 2011; Minozzi and Volden 2013). In particular, if political parties can structure the legislative agenda by controlling key veto points in the chamber as suggested by Cox and McCubbins (2005) or by buying off the loyalty of certain members of their coalitions (Snyder 1991), and individual legislators use spatial logic to make choices about which bills to support, then, under a reasonable set of assumptions about the location of the status quo, ideological extremists should be the most likely to support their party's proposals. The legislators least likely to support their party's proposals should come from the ideologically moderate wings of a party. Empirically, this seems to hold on for the US case (Kirkland 2014) but not at all in the United Kingdom (Benedetto and Hix 2007; Gaines and Garrett 1993; Kam 2009).

In contrast to models of US Congress, any model of voting and rebellion in Westminster must explicitly account for very high levels of party unity and a government-versus-opposition divide. Indeed, partisan politics dominates so much of the decision-making calculus of MPs that ideological voting is at best a secondary motivation (Hix and Noury 2015). Nevertheless, we see historical variation in parties' average levels of unity (Eggers and Spirling 2016), variation in individuals' propensity to rebel (Gaines and Garrett 1993), and that British voters value the dyadic link between themselves and their representatives (Bertelli and Dolan 2009; Bowler 2010; Cain, Ferejohn, and Fiorina 1987; Vivyan and Wagner 2012), including a representative's independence from the party (Campbell et al. 2016; Vivyan and Wagner 2015). This dyadic link appears to have much in common with accounts of representation in the US House (Canes-Wrone, Brady, and Cogan 2002; Carson et al. 2010), but it has received less attention in the House of Commons due to the strong power that parties wield in Parliament.

The relative rarity of individual defections from party-line voting in the United Kingdom and elsewhere has resulted in comparative and British politics literature that either (a) focuses on explanations for aggregate levels of party unity (e.g., Carey 2007; Sieberer 2006), or (b) has relied on issue-specific explanations for defections from the party line (Schonhardt-Bailey 2003; Berrington and Hague 1998; Cowley and Norton 1999; Lynch and Whitaker 2013; Heppell 2013). Theoretical literature on aggregate-level party unity in comparative politics has examined how institutions and government agenda control induce discipline among governing parties (Diermeier and Feddersen 1998; Heller 2001; Huber 1996), but less on why they might lead some MPs to rebel. The need to pass a policy agenda and the requirement that governments have the confidence of Parliament leads governing parties to demand loyalty from their backbenchers. Indeed, the literature on British political development highlights the relationship between government agenda control and party loyalty (Cox 1987).

It is certainly true that the Westminster system, coupling single-member district plurality elections with parliamentary democracy, empowers parties. Parties exercise significant control over candidate selection, and voters typically consider a vote for a particular MP as a vote for that MP's party. Nevertheless, an MP's name features prominently on the ballot, and MPs have a strong incentive to engage in activities that boost their name recognition among voters (Cain, Ferejohn, and Fiorina 1987). As voters value some degree of independence among their MPs (Campbell et al. 2016; Vivyan and Wagner 2015), rebellion is clearly one mechanism for generating individual recognition (Kam 2009, 113–117). As Kam points out, "British MPs appear to use dissent and constituency service as complementary vote-winning strategies" (Kam 2009, 103). The question remains, though, under what conditions is rebellion from the party an effective vote-winning strategy for individual MPs? We argue that the answer relates to MPs' ability to use their dissent as a mechanism to communicate policy stances to voters. In short, government backbenchers, and particularly those who stake out more extreme ideological positions, are better positioned to turn dissent into an asset than opposition backbenchers and moderates.

Beyond the United Kingdom, theoretical work suggests that governments can control the agenda to avoid legislative defeat if not disunity (Tsebelis 2002).[15] Theoretical scholars have paid less attention to conditions that might foster high levels of unity among the opposition (although Dewan and Spirling [2011] offer a model in which opposition parties can achieve more favorable policy outcomes by committing their MPs to vote en bloc). Others suggest that opposition parties may be able to avoid taking controversial stances on divisive issues in ways that governing parties cannot, leading the opposition to show higher levels of cohesion (Sieberer 2006).

Literature focused on legislative rebellion asks a slightly different, albeit related, question; namely, conditional on some existing level of dissent, which MPs are most likely to publicly rebel? In contrast to aggregate-level studies of party unity, this literature tends not to consider government agenda control as an explanation for rebellion. Instead, it focuses on an MP's ideology (Minozzi and Volden 2013), as well as the likelihood of promotion up the party ranks, and length of tenure in Parliament (Kam 2009). In the US Congress, Minozzi and Volden (2013) examine both minority and majority members, but do not specifically look at the interaction between being in the majority and party loyalty. In the United Kingdom, prior theoretical efforts to explain rebellion focus on questions of individual agency amid refusals of ministerial positions (Benedetto and Hix 2007; Kam et al. 2010; Eggers and Spirling 2016; Piper 1991; Tavits 2009), and as a function of individual ideology (Kam 2001), general socialization towards acquiescence to party leaders' preferences (Crowe 1986), strategic opposition to the government (Dewan and Spirling 2011), and constituency preferences on salient parliamentary issues (Schaufele 2014; Bowler 2010; Pattie, Fieldhouse, and Johnston 1994; Johnston et al. 2002; Longley 1998; Vivyan and Wagner 2012).[16]

3.3 Ideology and Grandstanding: A Theory of Rebellion

We provide a general theory of individual defections from party votes in which electoral incentives drive legislator behavior. We combine theorizing on

---

[15] There is an important distinction between the ability of government to use agenda control to pass policy and to reign in rebels. If a governing party controls enough seats, it is likely able and willing to bring a bill up for a vote (and pass it) in the face of some internal opposition.

[16] Recent work by Izzo (2018) has also advocated a model of individual dissent from parties as a way to motivate party leaders to adopt more extreme ideological positions, but does not make a direct link to elections.

agenda control – key to studies of aggregate-level behavior in both the American and British contexts – with explanations found in the individual-level literature to build a new theory. We consider how governing parties' commitment (and ability) to change policy interacts with individual ideology to generate electoral incentives for MPs to craft an image of independence through rebellion. In doing so, we contribute to the growing literature on representation and electoral signaling through legislative votes and speech (Maltzman and Sigelman 1996; Carson et al. 2010; Herzog and Benoit 2015; Proksch and Slapin 2012, 2015; Izzo 2018).

We argue that change in extremists' voting behavior when in government (or the majority) compared with opposition highlights features of British and American politics that the theoretical and empirical literature on parties and legislatures has largely overlooked, namely the link between agenda control, ideology, and rebellion. We demonstrate that rebellions are much more likely to occur among ideologically extreme legislators *when their party controls the legislative agenda.*[17] They rebel to signal ideological purity to an ideologically driven constituency. While differences in party and MP behavior between the US Congress and Westminster parliamentary systems are clearly substantial, we provide further evidence that these differences are more a matter of degree than of kind.

Our theory of rebellion hinges on a theory of elections and representation. As many before us, we view MPs as agents of two (potentially) competing principals – their party and their voters. Electoral incentives affect the degree to which legislators are beholden to these principals (Carey 2007; Hix 2004; Kirkland and Harden 2016; Lindstädt and Vander Wielen 2011). In both the United States and the United Kingdom, this tension can be made worse by the ability of individual members to leverage dissent for electoral gain (Campbell et al. 2016; Vivyan and Wagner 2015; Pearson 2015; Carson et al. 2010). We begin by laying out a general spatial framework, discussing how our model incorporates it, but also differs from it.

A large number of theoretical and empirical models used to study legislative choices assume a Downsian, or spatial, model of legislative decision making (Downs 1957; Poole and Rosenthal 1985; Ladha 1991; Rosenthal 1992; Clinton and Meirowitz 2001). When a legislator's own preferences are more proximate to the status quo, the legislator opposes the new policy, and when a legislator's own preferences are more proximate to the new policy, the legislator supports that policy.

---

[17] Specifically, we examine positive agenda control as found by Romer and Rosenthal (1978) rather than negative agenda control as in Cox and McCubbins (2005).

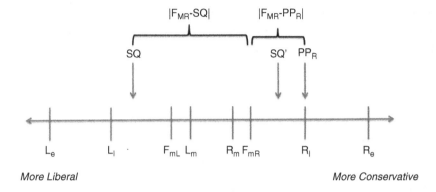

Figure 1: The Spatial Voting Model in the Presence of Legislative
Agenda-Setting

Figure 1 makes clear the assumptions regarding individual legislators' calculus
in these models. The figure presents an arbitrary left–right ideological space. We
locate two parties in this space – a party L on the left and a party R on the right. L_e
and R_e represent the ideal points of extremists in the Left Party and Right Party
respectively; L_m and R_m the ideal points of Left Party and Right Party moderates; and L_l and R_l the position of the respective party leaderships (assumed to
be near the party medians). F_{mL} and F_{mR} represent the positions of hypothetical
floor medians under Left Party and Right Party majorities, respectively. Thus,
we assume that the floor median moves left to right with a shift from Left Party
to Right Party leadership, and vice versa (a finding that Wiseman and Wright
[2008] have demonstrated both theoretically and empirically). SQ represents an
arbitrary status quo position located to the left of the Right Party leadership, and
PP_R is the position of a Right Party policy proposal when the chamber is under
Right Party control. Whenever $|F_{mR} - SQ| > |F_{mR} - PP_R|$, the floor median
supports the proposal over the status quo and it passes.

Let us assume that the Right Party has a majority, controls the agenda, and
wishes its bills to pass. Thus, the leadership only brings to the floor those
proposals that the floor median F_{mR} prefers to the status quo SQ.[18] Given

---

[18] In a unidimensional policy space, for a proposal to defeat the status quo, the proposal must be
preferable to the floor median of the chamber relative to the status quo. Assuming that party
leadership wishes to pass some legislation is tantamount to assuming that floor medians wield
some power in a legislature. Jenkins and Monroe (2012) suggest that to buck the preferences of
the floor median and bring non-median preferred legislation to the floor is quite costly for the
majority party. Additionally, vote-buying models of legislative behavior suggest a powerful
agenda-setting role for the median (Snyder 1991; Groseclose and Snyder 1996). More recently,
Lynch, Madonna, and Roberts (2016) also suggest that floor medians must either be satisfied
with proposals or bought off for those proposals to come to the floor in the House.

agenda-setting powers, the Right Party leadership select a PP_R as close to R_l as possible while still being supported by F_{mR} over SQ. That is, they find the policy closest to the party leadership's preferences that the floor median still prefers to existing policy. Under these conditions only moderate Right Party legislators can be more proximate to SQ than to PP. Moderate Right Party members holding ideal points to the left of F_{mR} would rebel because the leadership only has to satisfy the more conservative floor median. Extremist Right Party members would only have a spatial incentive to defect if SQ were located to the right of the leadership, causing the leadership to push for change in a moderate direction. In this instance, we would expect all members of the legislature, left-wing and right-wing, to support the Right Party leadership's proposal, except for those few conservative extremists closer to SQ.[19] Thus, for members of the majority party, we would never expect extremists to rebel on votes that divide the parties (where the majority of one party votes against the majority of the other), but we do expect moderates (those more left-wing than F_{mL}) to rebel on votes when their own leadership moves policy too far right relative to the SQ.

Now let us consider how spatial incentives change for moderates when their party loses the majority and agenda control shifts. The floor median moves left, from F_{mR} to F_{mL}, and the new majority seeks to move policy to left. Namely, they seek to alter policies with right-of-center status quo positions such as SQ'.[20] In the minority, only moderate Right Party members ever have a spatial incentive to rebel from their party majority – any Left Party proposal that Right Party extremists prefer over SQ' must also be preferred by Right Party moderates. Because the Left Party proposal, PP_L, only has to leave the center-left floor median, F_{mL}, better off compared with SQ', only Right Party moderates sufficiently left-wing to prefer such a PP_L would vote with the Left Party and against their party majority.

Moreover, for moderate status quo locations, the exact same moderate members who would vote against their party when in the majority support their party when in the minority. They do so by voting against change regardless of which party has agenda control. The majority party proposes policy that satisfies the floor median, not its most moderate members, leaving these majority party moderates worse off. However, the other party, if in the minority,

---

[19] Put another way, if a party is attempting to moderate an extreme policy, all of that party's moderates and all of the opposition party should support the proposal. Additionally, all of a party's extreme members closer to the moderate proposal than the status quo will support the policy.

[20] SQ' is an example of a policy that a right-wing party may have passed previously, and thus becomes the status quo inherited by a left-wing party when it takes control.

would move policy in the opposite direction, leaving both the moderates and the rest of their party worse off. Moderates close to the status quo will always appear less loyal in the majority simply by opposing change.

Spatial logic, coupled with Romer-Rosenthal-style legislative agenda-setting, implies that moderates rebel more frequently than extremists, who never rebel on votes that divide the parties (e.g., when status quo positions are moderate). And moderates rebel more often in the majority than the minority, also when status quo positions are moderate. It worth noting that moderate status quo positions are also linked to polarized parties. When status quo positions are moderate, most members of one party vote against most members of the other, making the parties distinct and in disagreement. If status quo positions were extreme, majorities in both parties would support change. Thus, this logic is strongest when parties are polarized.

Assuming moderate status quo positions, we derive the following propositions:

Spatial Proposition 1: Moderates defect from their party majority more often than extremists.

Spatial Proposition 2: Moderates defect from their party majority more often when they belong to the majority party than the minority party.

Spatial Proposition 3: Extremists are highly loyal partisans regardless of their party's majority status.

The first proposition holds in the US Congress, but not in the British House of Commons. But as the patterns in our earlier examples suggest (and the analyses in the subsequent sections will demonstrate), Propositions 2 and 3 find no support in the data. Instead, we demonstrate that legislative agenda-setting institutions controlled by the majority party interact with ideology and member strategy to produce patterns of defection where extremists rebel more when their party is the agenda-setter. These findings suggest that spatial logic alone cannot explain defections on roll call votes.

Two basic assumptions lie at the heart of our theoretical argument. The first assumption is that the majority party can pass legislation that moves policy in its favored direction and away from the position of the minority party. Thus, the majority party exercises a significant degree of agenda control and has the resources to obtain the votes it needs to pass policy. This is perhaps more controversial in the American separation-of-powers system than in the British parliamentary system, but we argue a reasonable assumption nonetheless. The second assumption is that ideological moderates and extremists connect with constituents in different ways

(Fenno 1978).[21] Namely, as members hold more ideologically extreme views, they become more likely to align ideologically with their party's core voters, and emphasize ideological positions. In contrast, members holding more moderate views tend to focus more on policy gains and less on ideological position-taking.

Extremists commit to an "ideological brand" to send clear, consistent messages of extremity to voters who agree with them, while moderates focus on policy outcomes and securing distributive benefits for their constituents (Grimmer 2013a, 2013b). Most voters do not possess a sophisticated understanding of ideological distance and legislative voting. They are unlikely to recognize or pay attention to nuanced movements in policy positions, but they can recognize a member's commitment to an ideological stance and they observe the benefits their district receives through their representative, particularly when interest groups and media communicate these actions to voters. Indeed, extant evidence suggests both that voters prefer uncompromising representatives and that excessive partisan loyalty can be electorally damaging (Carson et al. 2010; Harbridge, Malhotra, and Harrison 2014; Harden and Kirkland 2018), especially in extreme constituencies (Harbridge and Malhotra 2011). Thus, undermining ideological purity to move policy is a sub-optimal electoral strategy for representatives in extreme districts. Taken together, these two assumptions imply very different patterns of party loyalty for extreme and moderate members that depend on their party's majority status.

We begin by examining incentives for extremists. As members hold more extreme views, they invest more in their ideological brand, and any action that dilutes their message could prove costly, even if the action assists in moving policy in their preferred direction. Said differently, ideological extremists are likely to vote against legislation that fails to move policy *far enough* in their preferred direction for fear that they may be labeled as compromisers. The pejorative term from US politics RINO – Republican in Name Only – provides an illustration of this logic. Some Republican members fear being construed as insufficiently conservative or betraying conservative principles in their pursuit of policy victories. Extremists are more likely to be electorally damaged by such a label, thus their concern for position-taking should be largest. They may also take advantage of the opportunity to defect in order to force future party proposals in a more ideologically extreme direction (Izzo 2018). For these

---

[21] For ease of exposition, we discuss two types of members – moderates and extremists. Of course, this dichotomy is a simplification as members exist along an ideological continuum. The pressures we discuss are most pronounced for the most extreme and most moderate members. But they, too, exist along a continuum. In the empirical analysis we examine all members across the entire ideological space.

representatives, the position of the status quo is less important than the position of the eventual policy outcome, and they are prone to ideological grandstanding – that is, opposing legislation even if it moves policy in their preferred direction to signal an unwillingness to dilute their ideological identity.[22]

The effects that these strategies have on party loyalty depend on the ability of the member's party to control the agenda precisely because parties possessing agenda control are able to move policy in their direction. As an extremist becomes more certain that policy will change in her preferred direction, she cares less about the position of the status quo – it will change regardless of what she does. Instead, maximizing benefits from position-taking (either in terms of one's own vote share, or shaping future positions of the party, or both) takes precedence. In other words, as the status quo becomes less important, the extremist becomes increasingly likely to defect from her party majority to avoid the appearance of compromise on a less-than-perfect proposal. She gains electorally by maintaining her ideological purity and by signaling her willingness to stand up for her ideology in the face of party pressure. When her party does not possess agenda control, this same ideologue appears highly loyal to her party by behaving in the same manner. She opposes the policy changes suggested by the majority (or governing) party, but so does the majority of her own party because policy is moving away from them.[23] In the minority, position-taking and spatial motives lead to observationally equivalent behavior – both make the extremists appear loyal to their party.

Empirically, the behavior of moderates differs between the United States and the United Kingdom and for good theoretical reasons. In the United Kingdom, high party discipline, resulting from pressures of the parliamentary system means that moderates almost never vote against the party majority. Moderates are loyal partisans, often wishing to climb the party ladder with their eyes focused on ministerial positions (Benedetto and Hix 2007; Kam et al. 2010). They are also less likely to represent easily identifiable ideological groups. In the United States, moderates can and do get picked off by the other party on occasion, both for ideological and electoral reasons.

Moderates in Congress are more likely to obey traditional policy outcome-based spatial logic as their ideological brand is less important to them, and they are more susceptible to party coercion via threats and rewards. Following

---

[22] It is important to point out that our theory emphasizes extremists' investment in their *ideological* brand, not their *partisan* brand. In its simplest terms, we are asserting that the costs of appearing to compromise can occasionally outweigh the policy benefits of a proposal, and that the costs of appearing to compromise are increasing in ideological extremity.

[23] For the ideological extremist, appearing uncompromising in the minority simply means opposing the majority party with the rest of the minority party. Appearing uncompromising in the majority party requires extremists to oppose their own co-partisans.

Carson et al. (2010), moderates behave as if they are electorally vulnerable. When in the minority, their party does not need their support to pass a legislative agenda. Thus, the minority party places less pressure on their moderates, and the moderates appear less loyal. They may cast votes with the majority to take positions that are more in line with the median voter in their constituency, to claim credit for some legislative successes, for ideological/ spatial reasons, or to better position themselves to extract benefits from the majority party.[24] When in the majority, the party is more likely to need the votes of their ideological moderates to achieve the party's legislative goals. Accordingly, the party leadership leans on moderate members more heavily. Again, moderates attempt to extract concessions from their party, which now controls the majority, and to move policy in their preferred direction with little regard for position-taking or ideological purity. Thus, moderates' loyalty increases when they are in the majority because policy moves in a direction they approve of, and they are still trying to extract distributive benefits from the majority.

Thus, by assuming that ideological extremists use rebellion to connect with ideological constituencies, and incorporating utility from grandstanding into our account of strategic party loyalty, we develop a hypothesis that we expect to hold in both the United States and the United Kingdom, and at odds with extant spatial models of legislative voting:

Hypothesis: Ideological extremists are more rebellious on roll call votes when their party controls the legislative agenda.

A few short anecdotes show how this assumption (that rebellion serves to generate a constituency connection) and hypothesis (that extremists rebel more in the majority party) play out in both countries. In 2011, ideologically conservative Tea Party Republicans in the United States opposed a deal to raise the debt ceiling, the limit on the amount of debt the US government can carry under the law. Congress is required to periodically vote to increase the debt ceiling because, unlike in other countries where the authorization of spending would automatically imply a government's ability to raise the necessary money through borrowing, US law does not assume that just because Congress has voted to authorize spending that it has approved additional borrowing to meet spending obligations. Rather there is a ceiling on the amount of money the

---

[24] A great deal of legislative scholarship has pointed out that victories in the US House are often much larger than minimum winning coalitions (Groseclose and Snyder 1996; Wiseman 2004; Banks 2000; Carrubba and Volden 2000). These supermajority victories typically include the minority party's moderates, which help these moderates extract distributive benefits for their districts (Balla et al. 2002; Weingast 1979, 1994; Engstrom and Vanberg 2010).

government can borrow, which must be raised when spending means that debt nears that limit. As a result, Congress must periodically vote to increase the amount of the money the government may borrow or risk defaulting on US government debt obligations. These votes are especially difficult for Representatives espousing a fiscally conservative ideology, even though they, just like others in the House, do not want to see the United States default on its debt. Republicans, under Speaker Boehner (R-OH), controlled a majority in the House of Representatives in 2011 at a time when such a vote was necessary. Boehner put forward a plan to raise the US debt ceiling that came with more than $917 billion in cuts to government spending while only increasing the debt ceiling by $900 billion. Even though extreme Republican members should have preferred this plan to the status quo, many ideologically extreme members like Michelle Bachmann (R-MN), Todd Akin (R-MO), and Ron Paul (R-TX) opposed the debt plan as a way to demonstrate their commitment to conservative principles. Bachmann suggested that "raising the debt ceiling would be 'giving the Congress a license to keep on spending'."[25] Bachmann at the time was launching her initial bid for the 2012 presidential election and was seen as a leader of the ideologically conservative Tea Party movement.

In the United Kingdom, Phillip Hollobone, whose aggregate voting patterns we briefly discussed at the section's outset, rebelled in particularly open fashion when his party controlled government. He was even willing to rebel against his party on votes containing core conservative principles, saying that they did not go far enough. In 2013, he led a group of Conservative MPs to vote against the Queen's Speech – the annual statement of the government's policy agenda. It was the first rebellion by government MP's against their own agenda since 1946. Hollobone, along with three other Conservative MPs, instead put forward an "Alternative Queen's Speech" outlining policies such as bringing back the death penalty, privatizing the BBC, and banning the Burka.[26] Hollobone's own remarks at the time suggested that he used such votes to connect with his constituents, signaling to them his independent spirit and ideological purity, saying to the BBC that he rebels because his role is to "represent constituents in Westminster, it's not to represent Westminster in the constituency."[27] He was putting on a bit of a show to demonstrate to ideologically motivated voters that he cared more for their views than the rest of the party.

---

[25] http://money.cnn.com/2011/03/31/news/economy/debt_ceiling_debate/index.htm.

[26] Robert Watts, "Conservative MPs launch attempt to bring back death penalty, privatise the BBC and ban burka," *The Telegraph*, June 20, 2013.

[27] See http://www.bbc.co.uk/news/uk-politics-23958650. Last accessed April 13, 2017.

3.4 Existing Theory and Evidence

Existing empirical literature on party loyalty and partisan voting in the United States and the United Kingdom, while providing evidence of party influence over members, does not speak to the logic we discuss above. The existing American literature does not consider the effects of majority status on defection from one's party.[28] For example, Carson et al. (2010) examine the effects of party unity on electoral outcomes. They find that ideological extremists are more likely to be loyal partisans, controlling for electoral safety, and that higher party unity can be electorally costly, implying that parties are careful in selecting whom to pressure. However, they do not examine how these patterns may fluctuate with partisan control. Likewise, Lindstädt and Vander Wielen (2011, 2014) find strong support for fluctuation in party loyalty over time as a function of electoral and partisan pressures, but do not examine whether party control of the chamber affects these pressures. Lastly, Minozzi and Volden (2013) find that that party pressure affects extremists and moderates differently, and while they do control for majority status, they do not examine the interaction of majority status and ideology – specifically, they do not examine how individual member behavior changes when parties switch majority-minority status.[29]

Additionally, more macro-oriented accounts of party loyalty like Lebo, McGlynn, and Koger (2007) and Patty (2008) provide theoretical explanations for changes in aggregate party loyalty over time, but are less able to explain individual variations in party loyalty.[30] Similarly, research on conditional party government has demonstrated that a number of institutions might be used to increase rank-and-file loyalty, but this framework provides no reason to believe that these institutions might increase moderates' loyalty while decreasing extremists' loyalty (Rohde 1991; Crook and Hibbing 1985; Shepsle 1978).

---

[28] Lawrence et al. (2006) do examine an empirical model that interacts ideology with partisanship, but their primary interest is in predicting the frequency with which a legislator votes on the winning side of a bill, not with a legislator's level of party loyalty. Additionally, nothing in their models would suggest that ideological extremists become *less* loyal when their party obtains majority status.

[29] Minozzi and Volden (2013) do include fifth-order polynomials of their key independent variables, allowing them to detect nonlinearities in the effects of ideal points on party loyalty. But detecting nonlinearities in the effect of ideology on party loyalty is different from interacting ideology with party status to detect conditional effects of ideology on party loyalty.

[30] In particular, Lebo et al. (2007) suggest that the average level of loyalty within a party is a strategic function of the loyalty in the opposing party. Patty (2008) alternatively suggests that the average level of loyalty in parties is a function of the size of opposing parties. Neither of these accounts provides predictions about why individuals change their party loyalty over the course of their careers as a function of their place in the ideological distribution of their party.

In the UK context, Dewan and Spirling (2011) put forward a purely spatial logic that could explain similar patterns, but they explicitly reject electoral signaling arguments such as ours as a driver of opposition cohesion. Their basic argument is that, on an issue-by-issue basis, moderates in the opposition are better off in a policy sense if they can bind themselves to vote against the government. Thus, moderates in the government are a more likely source of rebellion. Their model would predict that the identical MP should be more loyal when in opposition than when in government. We view this argument as plausible, but not necessarily contradictory to ours. It is entirely possible that on an issue-by-issue basis some extremists are indeed "moderates," or stake out a position close to the opposition on a particular issue, and these are the issues where we observe defection. We would argue that even if the spatial story holds true, government MPs are still able to use issues to connect with voters in a way that opposition members are not. Moreover, our theory can explain rebellion in instances when their theory cannot – namely, we would predict defection among government MPs when they truly take an extreme position and the status quo is likely to move in their direction, as suggested by the Hollobone story above. A spatial model does not predict defection in these instances.

3.5 Summary

This section has offered a new theory to explain rebellious voting among ideological extremists in the US Congress and UK House of Commons. Although existing theoretical work on legislative behavior would rarely put these two chambers in the same category, we provide a model that can explain legislative behavior in both systems, showing that they are more alike than we might think. Indeed, we think of this as a general model. In any legislative system where members face electoral incentives to craft a personal vote, extremists will be tempted to defect from their party when it is in control of government as a way to show independence. This temptation comes from the need to balance partisan pressures with constituent pressures, a balancing act that opposition legislators rarely face, but one that governing legislators face frequently.

4 Party Rebels in the United Kingdom and the United States

This section offers empirical support for the hypothesis presented in the previous section. The analysis examines changes in individual-level voting behavior over time in both countries, focusing on the interaction between ideology and agenda control. We begin by examining how individual member party loyalty (or alternatively, rates of dissent) changes as parties move from possessing agenda control, to losing it, to gaining it back again. The analysis reveals that, on the margins, dissent on roll call votes follows the same pattern in both the US House of Representatives and the UK House of Commons; this is despite the fact that aggregate behavior among members remains quite different. Ideological extremists react to changes in agenda control in the manner that our theory suggests.

But we also know that the US and British systems are very different, with the main difference being separation-of-powers (the United States) or the lack thereof (the United Kingdom). Even if the majority party in the US House controls the agenda in that chamber, the prospects for actually passing legislation, and with it, incentives to grandstand, vary depending upon which party controls the Senate and the Presidency. Patterns of rebellion among ideologues in the United States may more closely mirror patterns in the United Kingdom only for some configurations of partisan control. We offer several hypotheses about how divided government might matter for the prevalence of grandstanding in Congress, drawing on what we know about both Congress and Westminster.

After demonstrating that partisan control of the chamber impacts dissent in both the United States and the United Kingdom, we explore the effects of divided government in the United States in greater detail. We find that the behavior among US House extremists most closely approximates the United Kingdom for the majority party under divided government. Under unified control, majority party extremists are slightly more loyal than under divided control, but less loyal then when in the minority. We believe that this is due to the shifting position of the majority party median under unified partisan control, rather than increased vote whipping by the parties.

4.1 Data and Models

Quirks of history mean that we can now examine the effects of agenda control and ideology on loyalty, whereas only a few years earlier these analyses in both countries would have been all but impossible. In the United States, Democrats held a majority in the House for forty years from 1955 through 1995. Only since 1995 has the US House experienced alternation in power. Moreover, because the House, Senate, and President have not all changed hands at the same time, we are also able to parse out the effects of different patterns of agenda control on rebellion and grandstanding activity.

In the United Kingdom, data limitations coupled with long-lived governments have made it similarly difficult to examine changes in individual behavior over time. But since 1992, we have both good data on MP voting behavior and changes in government from the Conservatives to Labour and back again to the Conservatives. Moreover, in both countries many members have served in the legislature long enough to have experienced at least one (and in many cases more than one) change in power. Using roll call vote data, we show that extremists in the United States and the United Kingdom behave similarly and they take actions likely to resonate with ideologically motivated voters.

We employ the same estimation strategy in models with very similar specifications in both countries, and we find very similar patterns of dissent among extremists. Specifically, we employ fractional logit models with MP-level random effects. Our dependent variable captures how often every Member of Congress or Parliament dissents from her party. Dissent is measured as a proportion – the number of times an MP rebelled from her party (or voted against the party majority) over the total number of divisions within a term – making OLS an inappropriate modelling strategy.[31] An individual MP's level of rebellion is properly viewed as a series of binomial trials coded one if a legislator rebels against her party on a division and zero otherwise. Fractional logit models take proportions in which the numerator and denominator are known and expand them out into sets of zeros and ones. For example, we may observe 100 instances of an MP opposing his or her party out of 1000 votes. This implies there are 100 ones and 900 zeroes in a binary coding of that MP's opposition to her party. From this setup a standard logistic regression emerges to predict the probability of an outcome, given some attributes of the groups (in this case, legislators), but with no information about the trials (in this case, divisions) themselves.

As independent variables, we include measures of individual-level ideology, a dummy variable capturing whether the MP's party is controlling the majority, and the interaction of the two. We also include a few standard controls in each case, including variables to capture electoral security.

4.2 Rebellion in Westminster

We begin by describing the results for the United Kingdom. We estimate separate models for two periods, 1992–2001 and 2005–2015, each consisting of two parliamentary terms. MPs who serve in both terms during a period appear in the data twice, while those who serve in only one term appear only for the term they serve. By incorporating MP varying intercepts, we remove the between-unit variance in rebellion and concentrate on the within-unit variance, meaning we examine *within-MP* change.

---

[31] More detailed information on the data, the data-gathering process, as well as a discussion of model selection can be found in Kirkland and Slapin (2017) and Slapin et al. (2018) and the accompanying appendices to both articles.

The tricky part of the UK analysis is obtaining individual-level estimates of ideology. Because party discipline is so high, we cannot use voting behavior as an indicator of ideology as US Congress scholars so often do. Instead, we estimate ideology based upon speeches on welfare-related bills using the *Wordscores* method (Laver, Benoit, and Garry 2003).[32] The estimates are based on an original collection of every speech related to welfare in the House of Commons from 1987–2007 by Tom O'Grady (O'Grady 2017, O'Grady 2018). The House of Commons is a good place to use speech data to measure legislators' policy positions because, as discussed above, British MPs enjoy substantial autonomy to speak as they choose compared with other legislatures.

We use speeches on welfare issues for both methodological and substantive reasons. Methodologically, by restricting the estimation to a single-issue area we avoid problems that may arise when speeches from several different areas are combined. Research on scaling speech has demonstrated that estimation of ideology from multidimensional speech can be quite difficult (Lauderdale and Herzog 2016). If the distribution of MPs' ideologies is multi-dimensional (for instance on economic versus social issues), then some MPs could accidentally be scored as centrist simply because they take extreme but opposite positions across dimensions. Likewise, with multiple topics, there could be a danger of conflating genuine extremism (a tendency to speak in extreme ways) with a tendency or requirement to talk a lot about topics that are relatively extreme to begin with. The latter is a particular concern in a parliamentary system like the United Kingdom, where some MPs are also ministers with formal requirements to speak about their own issue area.

Substantively, the welfare state is a controversial and highly politically charged issue that very clearly divides British political parties in a traditional left-right space, both between – and more importantly for our purposes – within each party. The Labour party originally created, and then staunchly defended, traditional welfare programs throughout most of its history. But under Tony Blair's leadership, it introduced significant welfare reforms that included cuts to major programs and the introduction of means-testing and "welfare-to-work" initiatives (Rhodes 2000; Clasen 2005). Within the Labour Party these reforms were hugely controversial and caused major internal strife, including the back-bench rebellions of Tony Blair's first term as

---

[32] We provide a brief description of the *Wordscores* estimation below, and a fuller description and validity checks can be found in Slapin et al. (2018). *Wordscores* works well in this instance compared with unsupervised approaches such as *Wordfish* (Slapin and Proksch 2008), which are less suited for capturing ideology from speeches (Proksch and Slapin 2010). *Wordscores* allows us to identify relevant reference texts to pin down the space. Additionally, by focusing solely on debate related to welfare, we ensure that we capture an ideological dimension that maps to a traditional left-right space.

Prime Minister (1997–2001) (Cowley 2002). Similarly, much of David Cameron's time as Prime Minister was taken up with far-reaching welfare reforms, which caused splits within the Conservatives, between the coalition parties, and within Labour as it struggled to articulate a coherent response. Finally, since *Wordscores* is a supervised algorithm, the choice of training data is crucial in estimation. Because welfare reform was such a charged issue throughout the period that we consider, it is easy to identify ideologically extreme factions that anchor the estimated scale, as we discuss below.

The speeches include both regular debates and scheduled question times for relevant ministries, including all questions to Ministers for Social Security, and a subset of questions to Treasury ministers that cover welfare issues. They were divided into two periods. The first runs from the 1987 election up to the death of John Smith, Tony Blair's predecessor as Labour leader, in June 1994, when Labour largely remained a traditional social democratic party. The second runs from June 1994 up to June 2007, the era of "New Labour" under Tony Blair, when it embraced welfare reform. Each MP is represented in one or both of the two periods by a single document, consisting of all speeches they made about welfare during that time. It is necessary to split MPs in this way due to ideological change over time among Labour MPs, who shifted substantially to the center under Blair. In our analysis, the 1987–94 speeches are used to estimate ideological extremity for MPs in the 1992–2001 period, and the 1994–2007 speeches are used to estimate extremity for the later 2005–2015 period. This division of periods not only corresponds to important changes within the Labour Party, but it also allows us to avoid issues of endogeneity as the speeches we use to estimate ideology largely pre-date the periods of rebellion we examine.

Finally, MPs whose total speeches about welfare comprised only a handful of sentences were discarded, as these documents do not contain sufficient information to estimate the MP's position. Because of this, and because some MPs did not make a single speech about welfare, we estimate positions for only a sample of all MPs who held office over the period. Nonetheless many of the most prominent names are included, both ministers and backbenchers, and there is very substantial ideological diversity among the MPs.

Wordscores requires the identification of reference texts. Our reference documents were chosen based on membership in MP ideological groups; they were not selected by pre-examining the speeches. For Labour, the left-wing reference document consists of all speeches made by members of the far-left *Socialist Campaign Group* during the pre-Blair era, when the party as a whole was more left-wing. It contains many famous figures from the Labour left, including Diane Abbott, Tony Benn, Jeremy Corbyn, and George Galloway. In total, 23 Socialist Campaign Group MPs were included in the reference document. On the right, we used speeches made by Secretaries of State in the later period who were responsible for the welfare state, all of whom were close to Tony Blair, supported welfare reforms, and were clearly situated on the right of the party (Alistair Darling, Andrew Smith, David Blunkett, Harriet Harman, and John Hutton). By definition, their rhetoric in Parliament supported the more centrist Blair administration.

For the Conservatives, the left-wing reference document consists of all MPs (in both periods) who were members of the *Tory Reform Group*. This is a moderate faction that has advocated for moving the Conservatives to the center, and is associated with socially progressive, pro-European views. Its membership includes a number of famous moderates, including Kenneth Clarke, Michael Heseltine, and Douglas Hurd, as well as MPs who defected to either Labour or the Liberal Democrats, including Alan Howarth and Emma Nicholson. The right-wing reference document contains members of the Thatcherite *No Turning Back* group. As the name suggests, this group argues for a continuation of Margaret Thatcher's conservative economic policies, and includes famous names from the right, including Iain Duncan-Smith, John Redwood, and Liam Fox.

The *Wordscores* measures of ideological extremism display statistically significant, albeit moderate bivariate correlation with the number of rebellions in each party and period. In Table 1, we present results from a multilevel fractional logit model with varying intercepts for MPs predicting rebellion as a function of party status in government, MPs' ideological extremity, and, critically, interaction of these two covariates. Extreme MPs generally rebel more frequently with the exception of the Conservatives in the early period. Most importantly, the interaction term across all models is positive and statistically significant. Ideological extremists in the Labour and Conservative Parties react to their governing party status in precisely the same way in both time periods; namely, by becoming more rebellious. These results also control for MPs' recent vote share, tenure, and leadership. Overall, our evidence strongly supports our contention that ideologically extreme MPs become more likely to rebel when their party becomes the governing party.

To facilitate the interpretation of the coefficients in Table 1, we plot the predicted probability of a rebellion by both moderate and extreme MPs for the

Table 1 British MP Party Rebellion as a Function of Ideology and Governing
Party Status

	1992–2001		2005–2015	
	Labour	**Conservative**	**Labour**	**Conservative**
Government	0.469*	−0.084	1.477*	0.307*
	(0.166)	(0.123)	(0.090)	(0.090)
Extremism	0.558	−1.672*	1.124*	1.448*
Score	(0.366)	(0.516)	(0.448)	(0.488)
Majority	−0.155	0.191*	−1.224*	0.138
	(0.102)	(0.104)	(0.143)	(0.161)
Leader	−1.123*	−0.753*	−1.015*	−0.877*
	(0.205)	(0.258)	(0.294)	(0.173)
Tenure	6.362*	2.758	16.556*	8.405*
	(2.187)	(2.583)	(4.217)	(3.116)
Gov't X	0.569*	3.398*	0.946*	1.109*
Extremism	(0.230)	(0.421)	(0.214)	(0.222)
Constant	−5.755*	−5.779*	−6.994*	−6.551*
	(0.271)	(0.197)	(0.332)	(0.319)
	N = 215	177	300	207
	LL = −677.422	−501.155	−889.254	−683.803

Note: Cell entries report coefficients from multilevel fractional logit model. Model includes varying intercepts for MP and Year. LL indicates log-likelihood. Standard errors are reported in parentheses.
* $p < 0.05$ in two-tailed test.

periods 1992–2001 and 2005–2015 in Figure 2. We differentiate within the plot between rebellion rates when these MPs are in government and in the opposition. As the figure makes plain, changes in rebellion by moderate MPs as their party switches between government and opposition are quite small in magnitude. In contrast, the likelihood of ideological extremists' rebelling significantly increased moving from opposition to government. Thus, in terms of both statistical significance and substantive magnitude, ideological extremists have strong reactions to change in governing party status that are in line with our theoretical expectations.

These analyses show that the most rebellious MPs tend to be ideological extremists who are more likely to rebel when in government. We suggest that this pattern emerges because extremists use rebellion to develop individual identities distinct from their party, helping signal a sort of ideological purity to ideological constituencies.

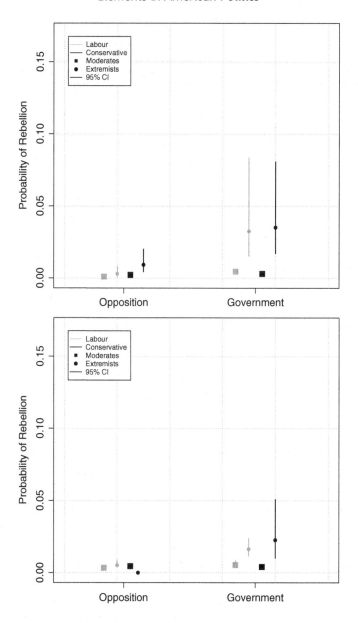

Figure 2: Predicted Probability of Rebellion by Moderate and Extreme MPs in Two Time Periods

4.3 Rebellion in the US House

In the United States, we explain party unity – the decision to vote with one's party – rather than dissent for the 95th (1977–1979) through 114th (2015–2017) Congresses for all members. The change in dependent variable reflects

Table 2 US House Member Party Loyalty as a Function of Ideology and Majority Party Status (95th–114th Congresses)

	Democrats	**Republicans**
Extremism	5.568*	2.953*
	(0.088)	(0.067)
Majority Party Member	0.550*	1.108*
	(0.209)	(0.097)
Majority X Extremism	–0.896*	–1.614*
	(0.048)	(0.038)
Constant	0.312	0.774*
	(0.159)	(0.073)
	N = 3659	2988
	LL = –20235	–16457

Note: Cell entries report coefficients from multilevel fractional logit model. Model includes varying intercepts for MC and Congress. LL indicates log-likelihood. Standard errors are reported in parentheses.

* $p < 0.05$ in two-tailed test.

the differences in how the British and American literature has evolved. But dissent is simply the inverse of loyalty, so we are still modeling the same quantities. Again, we employ fractional logit models. In the US case, we are able to better differentiate between types of votes, namely procedure votes and final passage votes. We expect to find strong effects on final passage, which typically only take place once passage is assured, meaning that dissent is almost certainly grandstanding rather than an attempt to kill the bill or alter policy, which would have happened at earlier, procedural stages. Table 2 examines all roll call votes rather than just final passage votes. We differentiate final passage and procedural votes in subsequent analyses.

To provide an exogenous measure of legislative ideology, Table 2 reports a logistic regression predicting the probability a legislator votes loyally with his or her party as a function of the absolute value of his or her lagged DW-Nominate score. Lagged DW-Nominate scores are highly correlated with contemporaneous DW-Nominate scores and are less likely to be caused by contemporaneous party unity scores. Thus, lagged DW-Nominate scores satisfy many of the requirements of an effective instrument for overcoming endogeneity problems in a regression context. We then interact the absolute value of a legislator's lagged DW-Nominate score with his or her status as a majority party member. Our expectation is that majority party status means very different things to ideological moderates and ideological extremists. In other words, the interaction of ideological extremity and majority party status should be statistically significant.[33]

To account for potentially competing explanations and the multilevel nature of our data, we also incorporate varying intercepts for each Congress and each legislator in our data. Thus, any variable that changes from one Congress to the next or from one legislator to the next is modeled in our fractional logit setup. For example, the ideological distance between the House parties has increased from one Congress to the next and the size of majorities change. These may in turn influence party loyalty, but the varying intercepts for each Congress account for this alternative explanation in our model.[34] Some individual legislators may come from particularly safe congressional districts, which also may influence their level of party loyalty, but again this alternative is accounted for by our varying legislator intercepts. We have also run models with a full set of covariates including seniority, freshmen status, a Southern state dummy variable, district presidential vote share, the emergence of a quality challenger, and others. Our results are unaffected by the inclusion of those controls and we opt to present the simpler model here. The full model can be found in the appendix.

The results from our multilevel fractional logit models in Table 2 indicate that as the absolute value of a legislator's lagged DW-Nominate score increases (indicating increased ideological extremity), the probability a legislator will vote with his or her party increases, precisely as the traditional spatial model would suggest. The results also indicate that this effect is conditional on a legislator's membership in the majority party. Because the models include an interaction term, the positive coefficient implies that when the absolute value of a legislator's lagged DW-Nominate score is zero (indicating a perfectly moderate lagged voting record), moving to the majority party increases a legislator's probability of voting loyally with his or her party. However, the interaction term is negative and larger than the coefficient on the majority party identifier. This implies that when the absolute value of a legislator's

---

[33] Using a lagged measure of ideology (lagged DW-Nominate) ought to allow us to estimate ideology from a set of votes unrelated to the votes for which we estimate party loyalty. However, DW-Nominate places strong linear restrictions on the amount of "movement" legislators can make in ideological space from one session to the next. This restriction implies that DW-Nominate scores at time t are closely related to scores at time $t-1$ by construction. This may imply that our use of lagged scores is insufficient to overcome our endogeneity concerns. We have also run models with new ideal point estimates from Asmussen and Jo (2016) that are comparable over time, but unrestricted in the evolution of legislator ideology. Those results mirror the ones we present here.

[34] We also take an empirical approach to studying the influence of party size on the distribution of party defections in the supplemental appendices to Kirkland and Slapin (2017). As we would expect based on our theory, as small (and thus minority) parties grow in size (and become majority parties), extremists become less loyal while moderates become more loyal.

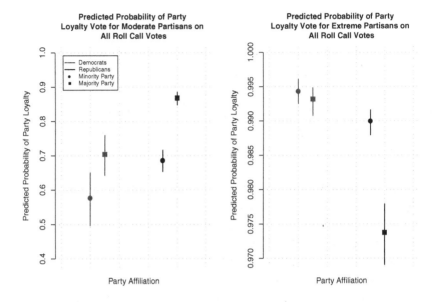

Figure 3: Predicted Probability of Loyal Roll Call Vote by Moderate and Extreme Members of the House (95th–114th Congresses)

lagged DW-Nominate score is one (indicating perfectly extreme voting behavior), the marginal effect of majority party status is negative; ideological extremists become *less* loyal when they shift to the majority party.[35]

To illustrate these conditional effects Figure 3 plots the predicted probability of a loyal party vote for a perfectly moderate and perfectly extreme Democratic and Republican House member in both the minority and majority party. The left-hand panel plots the probability of party loyalty for ideological moderates. For both Democrats and Republicans, there is a clear increase in the probability of party loyalty among ideological moderates as the party moves from minority party to majority party status. The right-hand panel plots the predicted probability of party loyalty for ideological extremists, and paints a very different picture. Democratic extremists become slightly (though not significantly) less loyal when their party moves to the majority. Republican extremists, however, become significantly less loyal when their party moves to the majority. It is important to note that the *y*-axes of these plots are quite different because the absolute defection rates are quite different for moderates and extremists. Nevertheless, the model suggests that controlling for any Congress- or legislator-level variance, ideological

---

[35] For Democrats, the marginal effect of majority party status for perfect moderates is 0.550, while the marginal effect of majority party status for perfect extremists is $0.550 - 0.896 = -0.346$. For Republicans, the marginal effect of majority party status for perfect moderates is 1.108, while the marginal effect of majority party status for perfect extremists is $1.108 - 1.613 = -0.505$.

moderates and ideological extremists respond to the switch to majority party status in very different ways.[36] Moderates become much more loyal, while extremists become slightly less loyal. This squares quite well with the expectations emerging from our theory of grandstanding and strategic disloyalty.

Because our theory suggests that much of this strategic disloyalty is motivated by an effort to appeal to constituents, a further implication of our theory is that these effects should be most exaggerated on final passage votes. Final passage votes, as opposed to procedural votes, are much easier for citizens to understand and they generally pit the majority party's proposals directly against the status quo. Procedural votes on the other hand, are rather obscure and less publicly salient, even if they are particularly important for legislative outcomes.[37]

Thus, we expect the patterns we observe in Figure 3 to be more muted on less salient procedural votes, and more exaggerated on more public final passage votes.[38] To test this hypothesis, we replicate the models in Table 2, but separate roll call votes into final passage votes and partisan procedural votes. Partisan procedural votes are roll call votes on procedures in the chamber intended to produce an advantage for the majority party.[39] Final passage votes are votes to determine whether legislation passes in the chamber. Each legislator in the data set receives a party unity score on both partisan procedural votes and on final passage votes, which is correlated with, but distinct from their party unity score on all roll call votes. Rather than report the model results in table form, from this point forward we concentrate on the more easily digested graphical presentation of our results, but full model results can be found in the appendix.

Figure 4 plots the predicted probability of party loyalty for perfectly moderate and perfectly extreme Democratic and Republican legislators in the majority and minority party using the coefficients from a model replicating the one found in Table 2, but distinguishing between final passage and partisan

---

[36] While the percentage point change in loyalty may appear small (less than 5 percent in some cases), the US House conducts roughly 1000 votes per Congress. A decline in party loyalty of just 2 percent implies an additional 20 roll call defections from a single legislator. We suspect that an uptick of 20 defections from a typically reliable ideological extremist would give party leaders concern.

[37] Partisan procedural votes are roll call votes on procedures in the chamber intended to produce a partisan advantage (like the motion to recommit). Not all procedural votes are partisan in nature (i.e., votes on the House journal [Patty 2010]). We use Crespin, Rohde, and Vander Wielen (2013) to categorize vote types.

[38] This strategy is optimal for both individual members and party leaders. Individual members can use final passage votes to score points with their constituents, while party leaders maintain loyalty on the votes that really matter. Party leaders accept some defection in order to help their rank-and-file win elections.

[39] Examples include votes on the motion to recommit (Roberts 2005) and the motion to order the previous question (Finocchiaro and Rohde 2008).

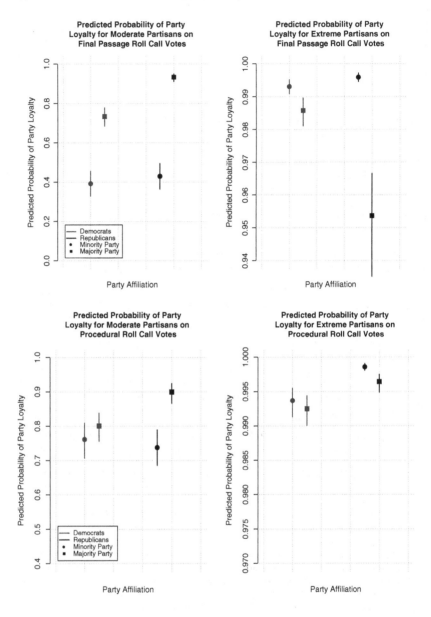

Figure 4: Predicted Probability of Loyal Roll Call Vote by Moderate and Extreme Members of the House on Final Passage and Procedural Votes (95th–114th Congresses)

procedural votes. The top panels plot these predicted probabilities on final passage votes while the bottom panels plot these relationships for partisan procedural votes. The predicted probability of party loyalty on procedural votes is essentially unmoved by transitions from majority to minority party status for either moderate or extreme Democratic House members. However, as we would expect, moderate Democratic House members become much more loyal on final passage votes as they move from minority party to majority party status, while extreme Democratic House members become significantly less loyal on final passage votes when they switch from minority to majority party status. These effects are more consistent for Republican House members, who see moderates increase in loyalty and extremists decrease in loyalty when they join the majority across both vote types. However, the effects remain much stronger for final passage votes than for procedural votes even for Republican House members.[40]

In sum, we consistently observe that controlling for any Congress-level or legislator-level alternative explanations, ideologically extreme legislators become less loyal when their party moves from the minority to majority party. Alternatively, ideologically moderate legislators become significantly more loyal when their party moves from the minority to majority. These conditional effects are strongest on the most public and salient votes, but they are relatively weak on obscure votes meant to produce partisan procedural advantages.

The evidence would seem to support our theory of strategic disloyalty and grandstanding. Legislators view final passage votes as chances to build their ideological brand, and are comfortable voting against their own party to improve their electoral odds. Because moderate and extreme legislators build different brands to court different kinds of voters, the effects of majority party status on their levels of party loyalty are quite different. The results also suggest that the policy implications of these defections are limited. Legislators are more likely to defect from their party on final passage votes when the legislative outcome has largely been assured. Very few House bills fail at final passage, while the most critical votes determining a bill's likelihood of moving on in the process are procedural in nature. Thus, these strategic defections are intended to produce a signal to a legislator's constituents of his or her distance from the party, without actually compromising the party's policy goals in a meaningful way.

Critically for our broader argument, we have now seen across several sets of statistical models that ideological extremists become less loyal to their parties when those parties gain agenda control, and ideological moderates become more loyal or stay loyal across that same transition. This is true in both the British House of Commons and in the US House of Representatives. Given the long history of scholarly distinction between these two chambers, the similarity in these behavioral patterns is striking. It suggests a commonality in motivation

---

[40] Each of the differences in the final passage vote probabilities is statistically significant at the 0.05 level, while only the differences in the Republican vote probabilities are significantly different on procedural votes.

for MPs in both settings despite stark institutional differences, a commonality we believe our theory goes a long way to explain.

But despite these commonalities across MP behavior, there remain some key differences in the design of the legislative chambers themselves. Perhaps the most prominent of these is the separation of powers in the United States when compared with the unified power of the executive and legislative branches in the British Parliament. One might ask, given the similarities we have observed between the behavior of members of Parliament and Congress, are those similarities consistent across the constellation of government types in the United States? Or are members of Congress *more like* members of Parliament under some conditions rather than others? We now turn towards examining the heterogeneity of our results across unified and divided governments in the United States to answer these questions.

4.4 Rebellion under Unified and Divided Government

While our analysis to this point has identified some common motivations for legislative behavior that we observe across legislators in these two environments, it is important to ask how these common motivations interact with differing institutional environments. To that end, we examine what constellation of government control in the United States makes American rebels most like their British counterparts. Given the United Kingdom's lack of separation of powers, one might presume that the US-institutional context most similar to the United Kingdom is unified control of government under one party. Under unified control, the majority party in the US House has a good chance of seeing its preferred policies become law. As such, the majority party during times of unified control must actually govern effectively. The party's opportunity to consider outlandish legislation, or blame an opponent for its failings is quite limited. With the pressure to govern in a responsible way, and the ability to actually do so, we might expect majority parties under unified control to introduce reasonably moderate legislation that only moves policy incrementally. Such incrementalism ought to generate *more* opportunities for grandstanding by extremists, assuming the majority can pass policy without their support. Indeed, it is easy to imagine ideological extremists in a majority party with unified control castigating their own party for its failures to do more, and with a long-term interest in maintaining party control, a majority party leadership that is comfortable with such castigation. This would suggest to us that ideological extremists in the majority party are *less loyal* during times of unified government than during divided government. Such patterns would mirror much of what happens in the UK system, where frontbench leaders are often chided by backbench extremists for their failures to take advantage of governing party power.

Alternatively, we could imagine that during times of unified government the party leadership in the House is allowed to move its proposed legislation in a more ideologically extreme direction. Freed from the need to negotiate proposals with the opposing party, party leaders in the House may see unified government as an opportunity to make drastic changes in existing policy, and to satisfy extremists' demands to do more for an ideologically extreme base. If party leaders use unified government control as an opportunity to enact more extreme proposals, then we would expect ideological extremists in the majority party to be *more loyal* during times of unified government than during periods of divided control. With more extreme proposals under consideration, ideological extremists will be asked to compromise ideological principles less often, and thus, have less reason to grandstand or be disloyal.

As such, we are left with competing expectations about how extremists' level of disloyalty ought to respond to their parties' transition from majority party of the House, but without control of the presidency or the Senate, to unified control of government. To test which of these competing expectations has empirical support, we engage in analyses of more specific subsets of our data and again employ our models from Table 2. We would like to see how the correlation between ideology and party loyalty changes across these transitions in institutional control. Thus, we again use our standard fractional logit approach, but instead of considering both majority and minority party behavior across many years, we examine the relationship between ideology and party loyalty in a few specific windows. We begin by examining the relationship between ideology and party loyalty among the Democrats in the 102nd and 103rd Congresses (1991–1995). In the 102nd Congress, the Democrats held majority control of both the House and Senate, but George H. W. Bush was president. However, in 1993, Bill Clinton took office, providing Democrats with unified control of government for two years. Using this specific change in institutional context, we can ask how the relationship between ideology and party loyalty changed as Democrats obtained unified control by regressing absolute lagged DW Nominate scores on party loyalty and interacting lagged DW Nominate scores with a dummy variable denoting Democratic control of the presidency. We again examine the probability of party loyalty graphically and reserve the specific results of our model for the appendix.[41]

---

[41] It is important to point out that Democrats are in majority control of the House in both of these situations. Thus, we suspect that ideological extremists have lower levels of loyalty relative to when they are in minority party status. The question is not whether our initial hypotheses hold (which we have already demonstrated), but whether we can differentiate between the behavior of majority party members during divided and unified government.

The results of this modeling exercise appear in Figure 5.[42] Across this transition, both on all roll call votes and on final passage votes, we see that ideological extremists become more loyal when their party gains unified control of government, providing some initial support to the notion that there are fewer opportunities for ideological extremists to grandstand when their party is in unified control of government.[43]

We need not just examine this specific change, however. Parties have had majority control of Congress without the presidency and then with control of the presidency at other times in our initial sample. In the following analyses, we repeat our initial modeling from Figure 5, but now consider both the Democratic Party and its transition from the 110th to the 111th Congress (2007–2011) and the Republican Party and its transition from the 106th to the 107th Congress (1999–2003). In the 106th Congress, the Republican Party controlled the House and Senate, but Bill Clinton remained in the White House, while in 2001, George W. Bush assumed the White House, granting Republicans unified control of government. In the 110th Congress, Democrats controlled the House and Senate, but George W. Bush remained in the White House, while in 2009 at the outset of the 111th Congress, Barack Obama assumed the presidency. These two transitions allow us to again examine the behavior of extremists under majority party-divided status and unified control of government.

Figure 6 plots the party loyalty of ideological extremists across these two transitions. For Republicans, the transition between majority party-divided status to unified control again results in higher levels of loyalty in analyses of both all roll call votes and final passage votes, mirroring our Democrat results in Figure 5. For the Democratic transition to Barack Obama, we again see that on all roll call votes, there is a strong increase in the loyalty of extremists when we examine all votes, but a decline in loyalty among extremists on final passage votes. Thus, out of the six analyses we consider (three transitions, two types of roll call sets) five of the analyses suggest that extremists become more loyal when their party moves from majority party-divided status to unified control of government. These differences are quite modest in magnitude. Indeed, many imply only a greater level of loyalty among extremists of one or two roll call votes, but they consistently point in the same direction. Thus, we are quite confident that extremists do not become *less* loyal under unified control, and if there is any movement in extremists' loyalty, it is an increase as their majority party gains control of the presidency.[44]

---

[42] We note in each figure when a difference in probabilities is significant at the 0.05 level.

[43] We define an ideological extremist in this plot as someone with an absolute value of lagged Nominate of 1.0.

[44] Indeed, these modest changes from majority party-divided status to unified control of government among extremists suggest that most of the dynamic change in extremists' level of loyalty occurs at the transition from minority to majority status, the transition that is the emphasis of our theory.

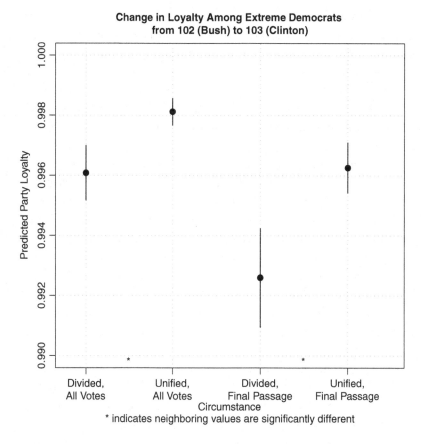

**Change in Loyalty Among Extreme Democrats
from 102 (Bush) to 103 (Clinton)**

* indicates neighboring values are significantly different

Figure 5: Predicted Probability of Loyal Roll Call Vote by Extreme House Democrats in the 102nd and 103rd Congresses

Pushing our analysis further, we can consider the implications for moderates, as well. If, as we have suggested, unified government gives the majority party a chance to effectively govern, we would likely see majority party leaders exercising more control over their caucus, in general. They may whip members into line and demand loyalty on all fronts. A demand for loyalty to enact an agenda ought to lead to increases in partisan voting among moderate members, too. After all, the party leadership is demanding loyalty from all members to pass policy before they lose precious unified control. As was the case for our extremists, ideologically moderate members of the majority party may also become *more* loyal to their party as it moves from divided to unified control.

Alternatively, if party leaders see unified government as a chance to enact more extreme legislation, thus gaining some votes from ideological extremists, their actions might result in less loyalty from moderates. Party leaders may push legislation even *less* palatable to moderates than they would under divided government. Lastly, for moderates, we have a third possibility. In our theoretical development, we suggested that moderates are loyal in hopes of extracting distributive benefits from their party leaders. The implication is that ideologically moderate members of legislatures care less about the ideological location of policy outcomes (moving the status quo in a more liberal or conservative direction) than do ideological extremists, and that moderates can be bought off in ways that ideological extremists cannot (a result supported by Morgan and Vardy [2011] among others). This would imply that while extremists may respond to the transition from majority party-divided status to unified control of government, ideologically moderates may simply have no consistent reaction to such a move. Unmotivated by the ideological extremity of policy outcomes, moderates' loyalty is driven by their ability to extract goodies from leadership. In this case, moderates might respond to party whipping but are unlikely to respond to moves by party leadership to the ideological wings. In many ways, this account is more in keeping with our theory. Extremists grandstand based on policy outcomes, while moderates are less concerned with the ideological implications of policy outcomes. To examine these three possibilities, Figure 7 recreates Figures 5 and 6, but for ideologically moderate members of the House.[45]

The three figures show that for the Democratic transition from the 102nd to 103rd Congresses, we have quite mixed results for moderates. They become less loyal when we consider all votes, but more loyal when we consider final passage votes. For Republicans in the 106th–107th Congresses, we see the reverse pattern: more loyalty on all votes and less loyalty on final passage votes. Finally, for Democrats in the 110th–111th Congresses, we see some small consistency: a decrease in loyalty on both types of votes. The evidence here is a bit ambiguous, but we can clearly discount a uniform increase in loyalty by ideological moderates; the party is not simply whipping its members more now when it has unified control of government. We interpret these results as evidence that either moderates are not consistently responding to this institutional transition, or perhaps weak evidence of a decrease in loyalty among moderates when their party takes control of the presidency after having had control of Congress. These two arguments are consistent with our results for extremists, and suggest that party leaders see unified control of government as an opportunity to enact more ideologically extreme legislation, satisfy a base of ideologically extreme voters, and move the status quo of policy by a large margin without facing significant institutional friction. Moderates respond to this action with either

---

[45] For this analysis, an ideologically moderate member of the House is someone with an absolute lagged DW Nominate score of 0.0.

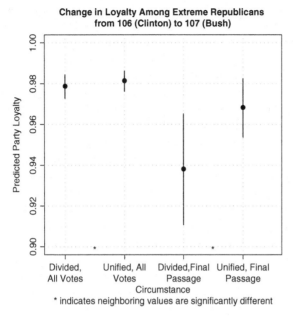

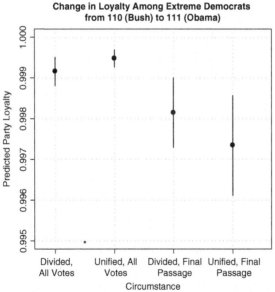

Figure 6: Predicted Probability of Loyal Roll Call Vote by Extreme Majority Party House Members in the 106th–107th Congresses and the 110th–111th Congresses

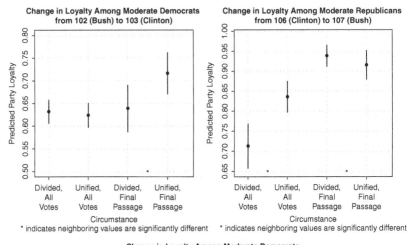

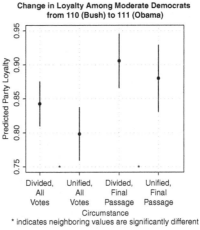

Figure 7: Predicted Probability of Loyal Roll Call Vote by Moderate Majority Party House Members in the 102nd–103rd, 106th–107th, and the 110th–111th Congresses

apathy (because they continue to extract things from leaders) or more disloyalty (as a reaction to the more extreme agenda of leadership).

So where does this leave us with regard to our initial question about which environment produces US legislators most like UK MPs? Our analysis suggests that ideological extremists are most loyal in the minority party (seen in our earlier analyses), second most loyal during times of unified control of government, and least loyal during times of majority party status, but without control of the presidency. Moderates generally seem to be most loyal during times of majority party control without control of the presidency, second most loyal during times of unified government, and least loyal when in the opposition party. In sum, the US Congress produces patterns of majority party loyalty most like those of British governing parties under divided government. In this circumstance, majority party extremists rebel reasonably often, and leadership allows such rebellion in order to make further electoral gains. Moderates, alternatively, are quite loyal. Similar to the backbenchers of governing parties in the United Kingdom, they may hope to parlay loyalty into leadership positions within the party.

4.5 Summary

Our analysis of MPs in British Parliament confirms that almost all voting defections come from ideological extremists when their party controls the government, an empirical regularity that British scholars have long intuitively known, but for which we only now have incontrovertible evidence. While on average American legislators behave quite differently to their British counter-parts, on the margins American and British extremists exhibit similar patterns of rebellion. Moreover, American legislative parties most resemble British govern-ing parties during times of majority party status when they do not control the presidency. This constellation of divided government produces relatively loyal moderates with comparatively more defections from extremists. The need for some compromise with the President to pass policy likely means the majority party must moderate its views on occasion, opening up the possibility that extremists dissent from the party line to signal ideological purity.

On the surface, this finding is somewhat surprising. We might expect American governing parties to most resemble their British counterparts under unified partisan control of Congress and the Presidency, a constellation that we might assume mirrors a single-party government. However, in practice, under unified control US extremists find it somewhat less necessary to rebel. It is difficult to parse out the exact reasons why. As we discuss above, we suspect that under unified control, increased levels of loyalty result from the majority party median shifting towards the extreme, rather than changes in levels of party whipping. Alternatively, with thin margins or insufficient coordination among members, extremists could be unsure whether they can grandstand, fearing that their rebellion may endanger the outcome of a vote. We leave it to future work to come up with a definitive answer.

5 Politics Today and Conclusion

The analysis in the previous section presents evidence up through 2017 for the United States and through 2015 in the United Kingdom. As we discussed in the second section, much has happened in both countries in the intervening period. In the United States, Donald Trump unexpectedly won the Republican presidential nomination and then the Presidency in 2016, turning the Republican Party establishment upside down. And in the United Kingdom, perennial parliamentary rebel and leftist Jeremy Corbyn became leader of the Labour Party in 2015, followed by the United Kingdom's vote to leave the European Union in 2016, a decision for which the ramifications remain unclear. Theresa May took over as Prime Minister from David Cameron following the EU referendum and then in April 2017 she called for an early election. To the surprise of many, the election resulted in her party losing seats and forming a minority government propped up by the support of the Northern Irish Democratic Unionist Party (DUP).

In this final section, we begin by examining how the political shocks we discussed in Section 2 are related to the theory and the evidence that we have presented in Sections 3 and 4. We then discuss how the politics we discussed in the previous section have changed in the last few years in both countries as a result of these political shocks. Finally, we discuss what our theory and findings imply for countries beyond the United States and the United Kingdom before offering some final conclusions.

5.1 Political Change and Grandstanding in the United States and United Kingdom

Even before 2016, we witnessed ideological activists asserting themselves on both the left and the right – on the right, we have seen growing support for the Tea Party movement (United States) and the rise of UKIP (United Kingdom); and on the left, we saw support for Bernie Sanders (United States) and the rise of the Momentum movement (United Kingdom), a left-wing trade union movement closely associated with Jeremy Corbyn. We believe these changes are closely related to the politics of "grandstanding" for which we find evidence. The changes have fostered conditions that promote "grandstanding" among ideological extremists, but also "grandstanding" may have encouraged further action among these ideologically driven activists.

Changes that empower ideologically driven activists, including alterations to candidate selection procedures that dilute party control (as has been the case for both the British Labour and the US Republican parties), encourage elected officials to engage in activities that pander to these ideologues. It is not surprising that both members of Congress and the House of Commons take opportunities to stand up to the party leadership in the name of ideological purity to speak directly to these activists. For members on the fringes of the party, it can be a vote-winning strategy. In the United States, incumbents could view grandstanding as necessary to ward off the prospect of a tough challenger in a primary election. But by engaging in activity that panders to these ideologically driven factions, elected members of Congress and Parliament may be further empowering and encouraging ideologues. Activists may press for more change to candidate selection rules or for more power to control the outcomes of the party conference if they see that their tactics succeed in getting their views expressed on the floor of the legislature.

Of course, the causes behind the rise of populist movements on the right and left – the Tea Party, UKIP, Momentum, Bernie Sanders, Trump, and Brexit – are numerous, including many we have not mentioned at all – the financial crisis, globalization, and immigration to name a few. But the dynamics of grandstanding in legislatures that we have uncovered could both result from these new political movements, and also fan their flames. We do not believe it is a stretch to assert that the changes that we have seen in both the United States and United Kingdom are related to the new similarities we uncover in legislative behavior.

5.2 Rebellion in the United Kingdom, Post-2015

The standard story of rebellion in British politics outlined in sections 3 and 4 rests on the assumption that the party leadership speaks for the majority of the party. Extremists rebel because rebellion allows them to differentiate themselves from the party mainstream. But what happens when the party leadership comes from the ideologically extreme wing of the party? Usually, any answer to this question necessarily involves an abstract thought experiment – while party leaders may hold positions that range from the more moderate to the more extreme, they usually can claim to speak for the vast bulk of their parliamentary membership. The election of Jeremy Corbyn as leader of the Labour Party, largely the result of a series of unforeseen and unpredictable events, means that one of the previously most extreme and rebellious of backbenchers is now setting party policy in Parliament.[46] We can examine how the party reacts.

In the roughly two years from Corbyn's first election as leader until Theresa May's snap election in June of 2017, the opposition Labour Party actually experienced slightly more rebellion than the Conservative government. The most rebellious backbenchers were not members of the governing party, but rather opposition backbenchers.[47] However, almost all of these rebellions came

---

[46] As discussed in Section 2, Corbyn's election was the result of the unanticipated consequences of changes to Labour's rules for electing a leader, coupled with the desire of some MPs to nominate Corbyn for the leadership to bring some diversity of views to the leadership contest, never thinking that Corbyn could actually win.

[47] Philip Hollobone of the Conservatives was the one exception. He was the most rebellious Member of Parliament in this period, rebelling 28 times. Labour MPs Graham Stringer, Kelvin Hopkins, and Kate Hoey all rebelled 22 times, more than any other Conservative MPs.

on votes related to leaving the European Union. Labour backbenchers supportive of leaving the European Union – e.g., Graham Stringer, Kelvin Hopkins, Kate Hoey, and Gisela Stuart – voted against the majority of the Labour Party 20 or more times. Despite Corbyn's own skepticism regarding Europe, the Labour frontbench preferred that the government pass Brexit-related legislation with their own votes. Disregarding EU-related votes for the moment, though, voting in the 2015–2017 Parliament looked much like voting in earlier periods. Ideological extremists on the government side of the aisle (e.g., Philip Hollobone and David Nuttall) rebelled relatively frequently, while the opposition, in spite of the tensions between the parliamentary party and the leadership, largely voted together.

We would argue that the deep ideological divisions between the new Labour leadership and the backbenches are not apparent on voting, despite being quite apparent in the press and playing out in several shadow cabinet reshuffles, because Labour does not control the parliamentary agenda. Corbyn cannot push forward his legislative agenda, and the backbenchers cannot express their opposition to it on the floor. Thus, the Corbyn era provides further evidence for our thesis. Even when significant shifts in the ideological position of party leadership lead to large ideological divides between the frontbench and the rest of parliamentary party, there are few opportunities to voice that discontent through voting when in opposition. If Labour were to win the next election, however, that behavior could change. It may be that when the leadership holds ideologically extreme positions, moderates rebel relatively more, making parliamentary voting appear more spatial and more like voting in the US Congress. We will need to wait to see if history gives us an opportunity to evaluate this hypothesis, though.

The United Kingdom's vote to leave the European Union has represented an even bigger disruption to the political system. In fact, the referendum, coupled with Theresa May's failure to capture a majority in the 2017 election has meant that parliamentary activity on anything non-Brexit related has largely ground to a halt. From 1992 to 2015, Parliament averaged approximately 240 divisions per year. In the first year of David Cameron's majority government from May 2015 until the referendum in June 2016, Parliament voted 290 times – a level of voting activity perfectly in line with previous parliaments. But following the vote on June 23 to leave the EU, levels of activity in Parliament changed quite drastically.

In the 12 months following the referendum until the snap election in June 2017, Parliament divided 177 times, roughly 16 times per month. In the 10 months from the snap election until the time of writing,[48] the pace of legislation

---

[48] March 15, 2018.

has slowed further to an average of only 13 votes per month. Of all the divisions held since the Brexit vote, a full 29 percent are on Brexit-related matters. The low numbers of non–Brexit-related divisions primarily reflect both government's unwillingness to bring policy to the floor given their slim majority and also the fact that preparing legislation to implement Brexit takes up a significant amount of time.

The focus on Brexit, the fact that Theresa May's government has largely adopted the positions of those members most skeptical of the European Union, and government's narrow majority has also meant that the patterns of government rebellion in the 10 months since the snap election have looked quite different. The usual rebel suspects – ideologues representing the social conservative wing of the party including Peter Bone, Philip Davies, and Philip Hollobone – are not the most rebellious MPs. These three have voted against the Conservative majority one, two, and three times respectively, no more than many other much more moderate members of the party. Instead, the two most rebellious Conservatives are the moderates Kenneth Clarke and Anne Soubry, the party's staunchest supporters of European cooperation. Thus, the politics of Brexit, coupled with the minority government, mean that the spatial model seems to explain voting in Westminster much better than usual. In very un–Westminster-like fashion, the vocal moderates are crossing the aisle to side with the opposition party, which espouses a policy position more in line with their views.

5.3 Rebellion in the United States, Post-Trump

The Trump presidency meant that Republicans controlled both chambers of Congress and the Presidency for the first time since 2007. The results from section 4 demonstrated that, while House extremists in the majority are still relatively less loyal compared to when they are in the minority, they become slightly more loyal under unified partisan control. However, we must ask whether unified control under Trump is the same as unified control under other presidents. Trump is certainly not a typical Republican president.

We find that under Trump, extremists become somewhat less loyal again. We identified the 10 percent most ideologically extreme Republican members of the House who both served in the last session of the Obama Presidency and the first of the Trump Presidency. This group includes noted right-wing House members like Brian Babin (TX-36), Jim Jordan (OH-4), Raul Labrador (ID-1), and Gary Palmer (AL-6). A quick look at levels of party loyalty among this 10 percent of Republicans reveals an average of 6 percent decline in party loyalty under President Trump's administration. Babin's loyalty declines by 2.5 percent, Jordan's by 3.1 percent. Labrador's loyalty stays relatively static, showing only a 0.2 percent decline, but Labrador has always been a relatively rebellious member of the Republican Party, voting with his party on only 90 percent of roll calls under both Obama and Trump (compared to 98 percent for Babin under Obama). Finally, Gary Palmer's loyalty drops 3.5 percent under Trump. While these percentages may seem small, recall that in any particular year, roughly 500 roll call votes are cast. Thus, a 3.5 percent drop under President's Trump's administration is akin to the ideological wing of the Republican Party defecting on 17–18 additional roll call votes with Trump in office than the exact same leadership (Speaker Paul Ryan's team) had experienced under President Obama. We would suspect that Speaker Ryan would find the prospect of Gary Palmer (a normally reliable member of the Republican Party) defecting from the House Republicans an additional 17 times rather concerning.

This decline is a little surprising, as earlier we found that extremists tend to become more loyal under unified administrations. Perhaps given Trump's extremism, the House Republican leadership has moderated somewhat, allowing space for extremists to rebel. It is also possible that Trump's divergence from the Republican Party on many issues has resulted in legitimate disagreements between party leaders and Trump, making the typical advantages of unified government for the majority less likely to be realized. Trump has consistently been at odds with both House Speaker Paul Ryan and Senate Majority Leader Mitch McConnell. Perhaps more likely is that President Trump's high levels of unpopularity (his presidential approval sits at 39% according to Gallup as of this writing) created a setting in which the Republican Party foresaw its large losses in the 2018 midterm elections. With the Republican Party brand sufficiently damaged by an unpopular president, and a number of retirements by prominent Republicans, ideological extremists in the party may be continuing to pursue a strategy of differentiation. By voting against the party *even more* than they had under President Obama's administration, ideological extremists may be attempting to distance themselves both from traditional elements of the Republican Party *and* Trump's particular brand of Republicanism. Thus, these defections could be an extension of the personal vote-seeking strategy that motivates much of our theory. Future scholars may look to test arguments like these by examining campaign advertising strategies or press release statements by ideological extremists under Trump (Grimmer 2013b). Examining the explanations for these somewhat surprising defections may tell us a great deal about congressional politics under a unified government, but with an unusually unpopular president.

The politics of Trump and Brexit in the last few months have meant that rebellion in the United Kingdom has looked slightly more congressional in nature while the US parties (or at least their extremists) look somewhat more

Westminster-like again. In the United Kingdom, government party moderates – those who prefer to remain in the EU – have been voting against their party, while extremists remain loyal; and in the United States, Republican extremists have started to grandstand at a higher rate under Trump.

5.4 Grandstanding in Comparative Perspective

Our core theoretical argument has been that in two-party systems where MPs benefit from building a direct connection with their constituents, ideology and agenda control interact to incentivize extremist members from the party controlling the agenda to "grandstand." That is, these ideologically driven MPs stake out positions that a particular constituency wants to hear by voting against their party majority, even if in doing so they are voting against a bill that might move policy in their preferred direction. We have argued that this model can explain voting behavior (at least among extremists) in the United States and United Kingdom precisely because these countries are both (primarily) two-party systems and because both members of Congress and Members of Parliament benefit from building up a rapport with their constituents.

For our theory to hold, it is important that MPs have an incentive to generate a "personal vote." When the electoral system means that there is little electoral benefit to MPs from building name recognition or an individual policy stance, then the MPs have little incentive to buck the party line to highlight their ideological differences. Thus, we would not expect our theory to hold in countries with closed-list electoral systems like Spain or Israel. Even in countries with more open systems, such as Austria or the Netherlands where the electoral rules allow for preference voting, the rules often make it difficult for voters to change the parties' initial ordering of candidates, or they incentivize voters to simply support the party ordering. We would not expect the electoral system to generate sufficient personal vote incentives in these instances either.

The two-party aspect of the political system is also important because it helps to clarify what rebellion means, namely voting in the same way as the other party. Our theory hinges on the ability of MPs to vote in the same way as the opposition without appearing to support the opposition's policy position (hence the importance of agenda control). In contrast to a two-party system, the meaning of rebellion in a multiparty system may be muddled. Imagine for the moment a hypothetical parliament with five parties, labelled A through E, arrayed across a unidimensional space from left to right. A majority government of the center-right is formed by parties C and D. In this instance, rebellion by a governing party MP does not have clear meaning. If Party C presses the coalition to move policy in a more moderate direction, some more-conservative members of D may rebel for policy reasons. They would appear to be supporting the position of party E over that of their own party. It would be difficult for the rebels to claim that they are truer representatives of their party's policy than the majority voting in favor of it. In other instances, government rebellion may come from more-moderate members of C who disagree with party stances more in line with the position of their coalition partner, D. They would appear to support policies put forward by B or A.

Because opposition parties lie on both sides of the government, government rebels cannot separate themselves from the position of their party without appearing to support the ideological position of a party in the opposition. While Republican extremists can vote against their party when in the majority and criticize their leadership for insufficiently living up to the party's ideals, the corresponding member of our hypothetical party D simply looks like a member of party E when engaging in the same behavior. The current situation in Germany following the September 2017 elections looks much like our hypothetical parliament. It will be very difficult for ideological right-wing MPs in the governing *Christian Democratic Union* to rebel without appearing to adopt the position of the populist right party *Alternative for Germany.*

Having said that, there may be occasions when our theory applies in countries with more than two major parties. When a single party controls government and there are no parties on their ideological flanks, opportunities for grandstanding may arise, regardless of the number of parties in opposition. For example, during the 41st Canadian parliament from 2011 to 2015 the Conservative Party under PM Stephen Harper was in government controlling a majority of seats. While five parties were represented in parliament, there were no parties occupying a position to his ideological right. MPs on the ideological right of the party could have rebelled and advocated more-conservative policy positions without appearing like the left-wing opposition parties.

5.5 Conclusion

Thinking about the applicability of our theory in both the United States and the United Kingdom in recent unsettled times, as well as in settings beyond the United States and United Kingdom, helps us to understand why the comparison between these two countries is so important. From an institutional and policy-making perspective, the US separation-of-powers system is quite removed from the Westminster parliamentary democracy. The US House of Representatives cannot form a government that controls the agenda. To pass policy in the United States, two legislative chambers and the President must agree. Institutionally, if we were to compare the United States to a parliamentary democracy, we might first think of Germany, with its federalism, strong bicameralism, and more powerful committee system. Indeed, research on comparative policy-making, such as Tsebelis's (2002) veto players theory, does just this.

However, we have shown that in terms of legislative behavior and electoral incentives, the comparison between the United States and the United Kingdom can be quite fruitful. Moreover, recent upheaval in both British and American politics, most notably with the vote to leave the European Union and the election of Donald Trump as US President, provides us with new and pressing reasons to compare how politics functions in these two countries. While much earlier work has compared the incentives to cultivate a "personal vote" in both countries (Cain et al. 1987), much less research has examined how these incentives alter legislative behavior in these contexts. Indeed, we typically think about the United States and United Kingdom as existing on opposite ends of the spectrum with regard to legislative behavior.

By carefully thinking about the incentives of MPs in Westminster, and then considering to which members of Congress these same incentives might apply, we are able to learn about the conditions under which members of Congress may behave like their counterparts in Westminster. We can use the same theory of electoral incentives and agenda control to explain the behavior of both. And perhaps surprisingly, we find that members of Congress are behaving more like their counterparts in Westminster. As Thomas Mann and Norm Ornstein have repeatedly pointed out before us, American parties are looking more parliamentary, and in the context of a presidential system, this may not be desirable.

Appendices

Appendix A

A Model of Congressional Rebellion with Covariates

The models in the main text lack many traditional control variables associated with models of party loyalty, and account for these potential confounding variables through the use of Congress-level and legislator-level intercepts. This approach controls for *any* potential confounding variable that varies by legislator or Congress, making our modeling approach more conservative than a model that incorporates some set of established control variables. Here, Table A1 replicates our results, but incorporates control variables that prior research suggests predict party loyalty. This model incorporates covariates for an individual legislator's seniority measured in years, freshmen status via a dummy variable coded one if the relevant legislator is a freshman and zero otherwise, a dummy variable identifying legislators from southern states, a dummy variable noting whether the legislators' district had recently been redistricted, a dummy variable noting whether a legislator's party was expected to gain seats at the midterm election, a lagged dummy variable noting if the legislator faced a quality challenger in the prior election, a measure of the lagged spending gap between a legislator and his or her challenger in the prior election,[1] and the lagged vote share of the presidential candidate from the legislator's party in that legislator's district. These controls come from both Carson et al. (2010) and Lindstadt and Vander Wielen (2014), which leads to a slightly shorter time frame for our analysis (stopping at the 112th House rather than the 114th). The models again include Congress-level intercepts and legislator-level intercepts to account for any unmeasured legislator-specific or Congress-specific variance unexplained by the covariates in the model.

Table A1 Multilevel Fractional Logit Models Predicting the Party Unity During Roll Call Votes in U.S. House Using DW-Nominate Scores and Control Variables (95th–112th Congresses)

	Democrats	**Republicans**
Lagged Ideological Extremism	4.613*	3.432*
	(0.125)	(0.142)
Majority Party Member	0.339*	0.960*
	(0.172)	(0.124)

---

[1] Campaign spending is logged and then differenced.

Table A1 (cont.)

	Democrats	Republicans
Majority X Extremism	−0.505*	−1.322*
	(0.071)	(0.071)
Seniority	−0.009*	−0.012*
	(0.003)	(0.005)
Freshmen Status	0.026	−0.009
	(0.014)	(0.016)
Southern State Identifier	−0.512*	0.324*
	(0.056)	(0.058)
Post-Redistricting Identifier	−0.042*	0.062*
	(0.019)	(0.020)
District Presidential Vote Share	−0.215*	0.335*
	(0.086)	(0.134)
Quality Challenger	0.056*	0.052*
	(0.012)	(0.012)
Spending Gap	−0.015*	−0.006*
	(0.003)	(0.003)
Midterm Party Advantage	−0.095	−0.075
	(0.057)	(0.080)
Intercept	0.697*	0.262*
	(0.159)	(0.117)
	AIC = 19867.3	14449.6
	N = 3505	2791

Note: Cell entries report coefficient values from fractional logistic regression models predicting the probability of party support by an individual House member on party-line votes as defined by Poole and Rosenthal (1991). Standard errors are reported in parentheses. Varying intercepts are included for each Congress and each legislator. Columns (1) and (2) report results for Democratic House members. Columns (3) and (4) report results for Republican House members. * indicates a p-value < 0.05.

Appendix B

Full Model Results Comparing Final Passage and Procedural Votes in the House

In the main text we break down the effect of ideology on party loyalty for members of Congress by votes on final passage versus votes on partisan procedural motions. Partisan procedural motions in the US House are motions designed to provide the majority party with an advantage. It is here that majority party leaders often most strictly enforce party discipline (Crespin, Rohde, and Vander Wielen 2013). Here we present the regression results that underpin the graphical illustrations of the differences in party loyalty by extremists and moderates on final passage and procedural votes.

Appendices

Table B1 Multilevel Model Results Predicting Party Loyalty on Final Passage and Partisan Procedural Votes in the US House (95th–114th Congresses)

	Democrats		Republicans	
	Final Passage	**Procedural**	**Final Passage**	**Procedural**
Lagged	6.201*	4.420*	4.529*	4.321*
Ideological	(0.187)	(0.169)	(0.152)	(0.152)
Extremism				
Majority	1.467*	0.230	2.924*	1.144*
Party	(0.176)	(0.183)	(0.184)	(0.182)
Member				
Majority	–2.540*	–0.464*	–4.226*	–1.654*
Party X	(0.121)	(0.088)	(0.105)	(0.094)
Extremism				
Intercept	–0.456*	1.159*	–0.293*	1.044*
	(0.145)	(0.151)	(0.137)	(0.140)
	AIC = 29483	46714	21620	32154
	N = 3659	3659	2988	2988

Note: Cell entries report coefficient values from fractional logistic regression models predicting the probability of party support by an individual House member on party-line votes as defined by Poole and Rosenthal (1991). Standard errors are reported in parentheses. Varying intercepts are included for each Congress and each legislator. Columns (1) and (2) report results for Democratic House members. Columns (3) and (4) report results for Republican House members. * indicates a p-value < 0.05.

Appendix C

Full Model Results for Sub-Year Analyses of the US House

We study the behavior of majority party members during three changes in control of the White House. These transitions moved the majority party in the House from control of the Congress to unified control of government. This analysis allows us to consider how party loyalty among ideological extremists is conditional on unified or divided control of government. These transitions include the Democrats gaining White House control in the 103rd and 111th sessions of the US Congress (Bill Clinton and Barack Obama), and Republicans taking control of the White House in the 107th session of Congress (George W. Bush).

Tables C1 and C2 provide the regression results that generate the graphics for our unified versus divided government figures. Interpreting these models directly can be challenging given the interactive specifications, hence our focus on the graphics in the text.

Table C1 Predicting Party Loyalty Among Majority Party Members As a Function of Ideology and Unified Control of Government (All Votes)

	102nd–103rd Congresses	106th–107th Congresses	110th–111th Congresses
Lagged Ideological	4.997*	2.913*	5.403*
Extremism	(0.166)	(0.265)	(0.325)
Unified Control of	–0.035	0.721*	–0.302*
Government	(0.026)	(0.052)	(0.043)
Unified Control	0.774*	–0.585*	0.783*
X Extremism	(0.098)	(0.108)	(0.139)
Intercept	0.541*	0.910*	1.678*
	(0.057)	(0.137)	(0.125)
	AIC = 3934	3329	3607
	N = 432	396	412

Note: Cell entries report coefficient values from fractional logistic regression models predicting the probability of party support by an individual House member on party-line votes as defined by Poole and Rosenthal (1991). Standard errors are reported in parentheses. Varying intercepts are included for each Congress and each legislator. Sample includes only majority party members. * indicates a p-value < 0.05.

Table C2 Predicting Party Loyalty Among Majority Party Members As a Function of Ideology and Unified Control of Government (Final Passage Votes)

	102nd–103rd Congresses	106th–107th Congresses	110th–111th Congresses
Lagged Ideological	4.327*	–0.009	4.026*
Extremism	(0.317)	(0.402)	(0.639)
Unified Control of	0.355*	–0.342*	–0.271*
Government	(0.070)	(0.161)	(0.113)
Unified Control	0.331	1.039*	–0.089
X Extremism	(0.244)	(0.302)	(0.327)
Intercept	0.571*	2.726*	2.263*
	(0.108)	(0.211)	(0.245)
	AIC = 2607	2075	2245
	N = 432	396	412

Note: Cell entries report coefficient values from fractional logistic regression models predicting the probability of party support by an individual House member on party-line votes as defined by Poole and Rosenthal (1991). Standard errors are reported in parentheses. Varying intercepts are included for each Congress and each legislator. Sample includes only majority party members. * indicates a p-value < 0.05

References

Aldrich, John H. 1995. *Why Parties? The Origin and Transformation of Political Parties in America.* Chicago, IL: University of Chicago Press.

Aldrich, John H., and David W. Rohde. 2001. "The Logic of Conditional Party Government: Revisiting the Electoral Connection." In *Congress Reconsidered*, edited by Lawrence C. Dodd and Bruce I. Oppenheimer, 7th ed. Washington, DC: CQ Press.

Alemán, Eduardo, Margarita M. Ramirez, and Jonathan B. Slapin. 2017. "Party Strategies, Constituency Links, and Legislative Speech." Legislative Studies Quarterly 42 (4), 637–659.

Bagashka, Tanya, and Jennifer H. Clark. 2016. "Electoral Rules and Legislative Particularism: Evidence from the US State Legislatures." *The American Political Science Review* 110 (3):441–56.

Balla, Steven J., Eric D. Lawrence, Forrest Maltzman, and Lee Sigelman. 2002. "Partisanship, Blame Avoidance, and the Distribution of Legislative Pork." *American Journal of Political Science* 46 (3). JSTOR:515–25.

Banks, Jeffrey S. 2000. "Buying Supermajorities in Finite Legislatures." *The American Political Science Review* 94 (3). JSTOR:677–81.

Baughman, John. 2004. "Party, Constituency, and Representation: Votes on Abortion in the British House of Commons." Public Choice 120 (1–2). Springer:63–85.

Benedetto, Giacomo, and Simon Hix. 2007. "The Rejected, the Ejected, and the Dejected: Explaining Government Rebels in the 2001–2005 British House of Commons." *Comparative Political Studies* 40 (7):755–81.

Berrington, Hugh, and Rod Hague. 1998. "Europe, Thatcherism and Traditionalism: Opinion, Rebellion and the Maastricht Treaty in the Backbench Conservative Party, 1992–1994." *West European Politics* 21 (1). Taylor & Francis:44–71.

Bertelli, Anthony M., and Rachel M. Dolan. 2009. "The Demand and Supply of Parliamentary Policy Advocacy: Evidence from UK Health Policy, 1997–2005." *Government and Opposition* 44 (3). Wiley Online Library: 219–42.

Binder, Sarah A. 1996. "The Partisan Basis of Procedural Choice: Allocating Parliamentary Rights in the House, 1789–1991." *The American Political Science Review* 90 (1):8–20.

   1997. *Minority Rights, Majority Rule: Partisanship and the Development of Congress.* Cambridge, MA: Cambridge University Press.

Bowler, Shaun. 2010. "Private Members' Bills in the UK Parliament: Is There an 'Electoral Connection'?" *The Journal of Legislative Studies* 16 (4). Taylor & Francis:476–94.

Bütikofer, Sarah, and Simon Hug. 2015. "Strategic Behavior in Parliament." *Journal of Legislative Studies* 21 (3):295–322.

Cain, Bruce, John Ferejohn, and Morris Fiorina. 1987. *The Personal Vote: Constituency Service and Electoral Independence.* Harvard University Press.

Campbell, Rosie, Philip Cowley, Nick Vivyan, and Markus Wagner. 2016. "*Legislator Dissent as a Valence Signal.*" *British Journal of Political Science.*

Canes-Wrone, Brandice, David W. Brady, and John F. Cogan. 2002. "Out of Step, Out of Office: Electoral Accountability and House Members' Voting." *The American Political Science Review* 96 (1):127–40.

Carey, J. M. 2007. "Competing Principals, Political Institutions, and Party Unity in Legislative Voting." *American Journal of Political Science* 51 (1). Wiley Online Library:92–107.

Carey, John M. 2009. *Legislative Voting and Accountability.* Cambridge University Press.

Carey, John, and Matthew Shugart. 1995. "Incentives to Cultivate a Personal Vote: A Rank Ordering of Electoral Formulas." *Electoral Studies* 14 (4): 417–39.

Carroll, Royce, Jeffrey B. Lewis, James Lo, Keith T. Poole, and Howard Rosenthal. 2013. "The Structure of Utility in Spatial Models of Voting." *American Journal of Political Science* 57 (4):1008–28.

Carrubba, Clifford J., and Craig Volden. 2000. "Coalitional Politics and Logrolling in Legislative Institutions." *American Journal of Political Science* 44 (2). JSTOR:261–77.

Carson, Jamie L., Greg Koger, Matthew J. Lebo, and Ernest Young. 2010. "The Electoral Costs of Party Loyalty in Congress." *American Journal of Political Science,* 54 (3):598–616.

Clarke, Andrew J., Jenkins, Jeffrey A., and Monroe, Nathan W. 2017. "From Rolls to Disappointments: Examining the Other Source of Majority Party Failure in Congress." *Political Research Quarterly,* 70(1): 82–97.

Clarke, Harold D., Matthew Goodwin, and Paul Whitely. 2017. *Brexit.* Cambridge University Press.

Clasen, Jochen. 2005. *Reforming European Welfare States: Germany and the United Kingdom Compared.* Oxford University Press.

Clinton, Joshua, Simon Jackman, and Douglas Rivers. 2004. "The Statistical Analysis of Roll Call Voting: A Unified Approach." *The American Political Science Review* 98 (2):355–70.

Clinton, Joshua D., and Meirowitz, Adam. 2001. "Agenda Constrained Legislator Ideal Points and the Spatial Voting Model." *Political Analysis*, 9(3): 242–259.

Cohen, Marty, David Karol, Hans Noel, and John Zaller. 2008. *The Party Decides: Presidential Nominations Before and After Reform*. Chicago, IL: University of Chicago Press.

Cowley, Philip. 2002. *Revolts and Rebellions: Parliamentary Voting under Blair*. London, United Kingdom: Politico's Publishing.

Cowley, Philip, and Philip Norton. 1999. "Rebels and Rebellions: Conservative MPs in the 1992 Parliament." *British Journal of Politics and International Relations* 1 (1). Wiley Online Library:84–105.

Cox, Gary W. 1987. *The Efficient Secret: The Cabinet and the Development of Political Parties in Victorian England*. Cambridge University Press.

Cox, Gary W., and Mathew D. McCubbins. 1993. *Legislative Leviathan: Party Government in the House*. Berkeley, CA: University of California Press.

2005. *Setting the Agenda: Responsible Party Government in the US House of Representatives*. New York, NY: Cambridge University Press.

Crespin, Michael H., David W. Rohde, and Ryan J. Vander Wielen. 2013. "Measuring Variations in Party Unity Voting: An Assessment of Agenda Effects." *Party Politics* 19(3) 432–457.

Crook, Sara Brandes, and John R. Hibbing. 1985. "Congressional Reform and Party Discipline: The Effects of Changes in the Seniority System on Party Loyalty in the US House of Representatives." *British Journal of Political Science* 15 (02). Cambridge University Press:207–26.

Crowe, Edward. 1986. "The Web of Authority: Party Loyalty and Social Control in the British House of Commons." *Legislative Studies Quarterly*. 161–85.

Denzau, Arthur, and Robert Mackay. 1983. "Gatekeeping and Monopoly Power of Committees: An Analysis of Sincere and Sophisticated Behavior. *American Journal of Political Science* 27(4): 740–761.

Dewan, Torun, and Arthur Spirling. 2011. "Strategic Opposition and Government Cohesion in Westminster Democracies." *The American Political Science Review* 105 (2):337–58.

Diermeier, Daniel. 2014. "Formal Models of Legislatures." In *The Oxford Handbook of Legislative Studies*, edited by Shane Martin, Thomas Saalfeld, and Kaare Strom. Oxford University Press.

Diermeier, Daniel, and Timothy J. Feddersen. 1998. "Cohesion in Legislatures and the Vote of Confidence Procedure." *The American Political Science Review* 92 (3):611–21.

Downs, Anthony. 1957. *An Economic Theory of Democracy*. New York, NY: Harper and Row.

Eggers, Andrew C., and Arthur Spirling. 2016. "Party Cohesion in Westminster Systems: Inducements, Replacement and Discipline in the House of Commons, 1836–1910." *British Journal of Political Science* 46 (3):567–89.

Engstrom, Erik J., and Georg Vanberg. 2010. "Assessing the Allocation of Pork: Evidence from Congressional Earmarks." *American Politics Research* 38 (6). SAGE Publications:959–85.

Esping-Andersen, Gosta. 1990. *Three Worlds of Welfare Capitalism*. Princeton University Press.

Fenno, Richard F. 1978. *Home Style: House Members in Their Districts*. Boston, MA: Little, Brown.

Finocchiaro, Charles J., and David W. Rohde. 2008. "War for the Floor: Partisan Theory and Agenda Control in the U.S. House of Representatives." *Legislative Studies Quarterly* 33 (1). Wiley Online Library:35–61.

Franken, Al. 2017. *Al Franken, Giant of the Senate*. Grand Central Publishing.

Gaines, Brian J., and Geoffrey Garrett. 1993. "The Calculus of Dissent: Party Discipline in the British Labour Government, 1974–1979." *Political Behavior* 15 (2):113–35.

Grimmer, Justin. 2013a. "Appropriators Not Position Takers: The Distorting Effects of Electoral Incentives on Congressional Representation." *American Journal of Political Science* 57 (3):624–42.

2013b. *Representational Style in Congress: What Legislators Say and Why It Matters*. New York, NY: Cambridge University Press.

Groseclose, Tim, and James N. Snyder. 1996. "Buying Supermajorities." *The American Political Science Review* 90 (2):303–15.

Hall, Peter, and David Soskice. 2001. "An Introduction to Varieties of Capitalism." In *Varieties of Capitalism*, edited by Peter Hall and David Soskice, 1–70. Cambridge University Press.

Harbridge, Laurel, and Neil Malhotra. 2011. "Electoral Incentives and Partisan Conflict in Congress: Evidence from Survey Experiments." *American Journal of Political Science* 55 (3). Wiley Online Library:494–510.

Harbridge, Laurel, Neil Malhotra, and Brian F. Harrison. 2014. "Public Preferences for Bipartisanship in the Policymaking Process." *Legislative Studies Quarterly* 39 (3). Wiley Online Library:327–55.

Harden, Jeffrey J. and Kirkland, Justin H. 2018. *Indecision in American Legislatures*. Ann Arbor, MI: University of Michigan Press.

Heller, William B. 2001. "Making Policy Stick: Why the Government Gets What It Wants in Multiparty Parliaments." *American Journal of Political Science* 45 (4):780–98.

Heppell, Timothy. 2013. "Cameron and Liberal Conservatism: Attitudes within the Parliamentary Conservative Party and Conservative Ministers." *British Journal of Politics and International Relations* 15 (3). Wiley Online Library:340–61.

Herzog, Alexander, and Kenneth Benoit. 2015. "The Most Unkindest Cuts: Speaker Selection and Expressed Government Dissent during Economic Crisis." *The Journal of Politics* 77 (4):1157–75.

Hix, Simon. 2004. "Electoral Institutions and Legislative Behavior – Explaining Voting Defection in the European Parliament." *World Politics* 56 (2):194–223.

Hix, Simon, and Abdul Noury. 2015. "Government-Opposition or Left-Right? The Institutional Determinants of Voting in Legislatures." *Political Science Research and Methods*. Cambridge University Press, 1–25.

Huber, John. 1996. "The Vote of Confidence in Parliamentary Democracies." *The American Political Science Review* 90 (2):269–82.

Izzo, Federica. 2018. "With Friends Like These, Who Needs Enemies." Working Paper.

Jenkins, Jeffrey A., and Nathan W. Monroe. 2012. "Buying Negative Agenda Control in the US House." *American Journal of Political Science*, *56*(4): 897–912.

Johnston, Ron, Philip Cowley, Charles Pattie, and Mark Stuart. 2002. "Voting in the House or Wooing the Voters at Home: Labour MPs and the 2001 General Election Campaign." *Journal of Legislative Studies* 8 (2). Taylor & Francis:9–22.

Kam, Christopher. 2001. "Do Ideological Preferences Explain Parliamentary Behavior? Evidence from Great Britain and Canada." *Journal of Legislative Studies* 7 (4). Taylor & Francis:89–126.

2009. *Party Discipline and Parliamentary Politics*. New York, NY: Cambridge University Press.

Kam, Christopher, William T. Bianco, Itai Sened, and Regina Smyth. 2010. "Ministerial Selection and Intraparty Organization in the Contemporary British Parliament." *The American Political Science Review* 104 (2). Cambridge University Press:289–306.

Kiewiet, D. Roderick, and Mathew D. McCubbins. 1991. *The Logic of Delegation: Congressional Parties and the Appropriations Process*. Chicago: University of Chicago Press.

King, Anthony. 2015. *Who Governs Britain?* Volume 7 of Pelican introduction. United Kingdom: Pelican Books.

King, Gary, and Andrew Gelman. 1991. "Systemic Consequences of Incumbency Advantage in U.S. House Elections." *American Journal of*

Political Science 35 (1). [Midwest Political Science Association, Wiley]: 110–38.

Kirkland, Justin H. 2014. "Ideological Heterogeneity and Legislative Polarization in the United States." *Political Research Quarterly* 67 (3): 533–46.

Kirkland, Justin H. and Jeffrey J. Harden. 2016. "Representation, Competing Principals, and Waffling on Bills in US Legislatures." *Legislative Studies Quarterly* 41 (3):657–686.

Kirkland, Justin H., and Jonathan B. Slapin. 2017. "Ideology and Strategic Party Disloyalty in the US Congress." *Electoral Studies* 49 (1):26–37.

Kitschelt, Herbert. 2000. "Linkages Between Citizens and Politicians in Democratic Polities." *Comparative Political Studies* 33 (6/7):845–79.

Krehbiel, Keith. 1993. "Where's the Party?" *British Journal of Political Science* 23 (2):235–66.

1998. *Pivotal Politics: A Theory of U.S. Lawmaking*. Chicago, IL: University of Chicago Press.

2000. "Party Discipline and Measures of Partisanship." *American Journal of Political Science* 44 (2):206–21.

Krehbiel, Keith, Adam Meirowitz, and Thomas Romer. 2005. "Parties in Elections, Parties in Government, and Partisan Bias." *Political Analysis: An Annual Publication of the Methodology Section of the American Political Science Association* 13 (2):113–38.

Krehbiel, Keith, Adam Meirowitz, and Alan E. Wiseman. 2015. "A Theory of Competitive Partisan Lawmaking." *Political Science Research and Methods* 3(3): 423–448.

Krehbiel, Keith, Kenneth A. Shepsle, and Barry R. Weingast. 1987. "Why Are Congressional Committees Powerful?" *The American Political Science Review* 81 (3):929–45.

Ladha, Krishna K. 1991. "A Spatial Model of Legislative Voting with Perceptual Error." *Public Choice*, *68*(1–3): 151–174.

Lauderdale, Benjamin E., and Alexander Herzog. 2016. "Measuring Political Positions from Legislative Speech." *Political Analysis: An Annual Publication of the Methodology Section of the American Political Science Association* 24 (3):374–94.

Laver, Michael, Kenneth Benoit, and John Garry. 2003. "Extracting Policy Positions from Political Texts Using Words as Data." *The American Political Science Review* 97 (2):311–31.

Laver, Michael, and Kenneth A. Shepsle. 1996. *Making and Breaking Governments: Cabinets and Legislatures in Parliamentary Democracies*. Cambridge, United Kingdom: Cambridge University Press.

Lawrence, Eric D., Forrest Maltzman, and Steven S. Smith. 2006. "Who Wins? Party Effects in Legislative Voting." *Legislative Studies Quarterly* 31 (6):33–69.

Lebo, M. J., A. J. McGlynn, and G. Koger. 2007. "Strategic Party Government: Party Influence in Congress, 1789–2000." *American Journal of Political Science* 51 (3). Wiley Online Library:464–81.

Lijphart, Arend. 1999. *Patterns of Democracy*. Yale University Press.

Lindstädt, René, and Ryan J. Vander Wielen. 2011. "Timely Shirking: Time Dependent Monitoring and Its Effects on Legislative Behavior in the U.S. Senate." *Public Choice* 148 (1):119–48.

2014. "Dynamic Elite Partisanship: Party Loyalty and Agenda Setting in the US House." *British Journal of Political Science* 44 (4):741–72.

Longley, Neil. 1998. "Legislative Systems with Absolute Party Discipline: Implications for the Agency Theory Approach to the Constituent-Legislator Link." *Public Choice* 97 (1–2). Springer:121–41.

Lynch, Michael S., Anthony J. Madonna, and Jason M. Roberts. 2016. "The Cost of Majority-Party Bias: Amending Activity under Structured Rules." *Legislative Studies Quarterly 41*(3): 633–655.

Lynch, Philip, and Richard Whitaker. 2013. "Where There Is Discord, Can They Bring Harmony? Managing Intra-Party Dissent on European Integration in the Conservative Party." *British Journal of Politics and International Relations* 15 (3). Wiley Online Library:317–39.

Maltzman, Forrest, and Lee Sigelman. 1996. "The Politics of Talk: Unconstrained Floor Time in the US House of Representatives." *The Journal of Politics* 58 (3):810–21.

Mann, Thomas E., and Norman J. Ornstein. 2012. *It's Even Worse than It Looks: How the American Constitutional System Collided with the New Politics of Extremism*. Basic Books.

Martin, Shane. 2011. "Using Parliamentary Questions to Measure Constituency Focus: An Application to the Irish Case." *Political Studies* 59 (2):472–88.

Mattson, Ingvar, and Kaare Strom. 1995. "Parliamentary Committees." In *Parliaments and Majority Rule in Western Europe*. Palgrave Macmillan.

Mayhew, David R. 1974. *Congress: The Electoral Connection*. New Haven, CT: Yale University Press.

Minozzi, William, and Craig Volden. 2013. "Who Heeds the Call of the Party in Congress?" *The Journal of Politics* 75 (3). Cambridge University Press:787–802.

Morgan, John, and Felix Vardy. 2011. "On the Buyability of Voting Bodies." *Journal of Theoretical Politics* 23(2): 260–287.

Norris, Pippa. 1997. "The Puzzle of Constituency Service." *The Journal of Legislative Studies* 3 (2). Routledge:29–49.

O'Grady, Tom. 2017. "Recruitment, Rhetoric, and Reform: New Labour's Politicians and the Transformation of British Welfare Provision." PhD Dissertation, Massachusetts Institute of Technology.

O'Grady, Tom. 2018. "Careerists versus Coal-Miners: Welfare Reforms and the Substantive Representation of Social Groups in the British Labour Party." Comparative Political Studies. DOI:10.1177/0010414018784065

Pattie, Charles, Edward Fieldhouse, and Ronald J. Johnston. 1994. "The Price of Conscience: The Electoral Correlates and Consequences of Free Votes and Rebellions in the British House of Commons, 1987–92." *British Journal of Political Science* 24 (03). Cambridge University Press:359–80.

Patty, John W. 2008. "Equilibrium Party Government." *American Journal of Political Science* 52 (3). Wiley Online Library:636–55.

2010. "Dilatory or Anticipatory? Voting on the Journal in the House of Representatives." *Public Choice* 143 (1–2). Springer:121–33.

Pearson, Kathryn. 2015. *Party Discipline in the US House of Representatives*. Ann Arbor, MI: University of Michigan Press.

Piper, J. Richard. 1991. "British Backbench Rebellion and Government Appointments, 1945–87." *Legislative Studies Quarterly*. JSTOR, 219–38.

Poole, Keith T. 2005. *Spatial Models of Parliamentary Voting*. New York, NY: Cambridge University Press.

Poole, Keith T., and Howard Rosenthal. 1985. "A Spatial Model for Legislative Roll Call Analysis." *American Journal of Political Science* 29 (2):357–84.

1997. *Congress: A Political-Economic History of Roll Call Voting*. New York: Oxford University Press.

Poole, Keith T., and Howard Rosenthal. 1991. "Patterns of Congressional Voting." *American Journal of Political Science*, 35(1) 228–278.

Proksch, Sven-Oliver, and Jonathan B. Slapin. 2010. "Position Taking in European Parliament Speeches." *British Journal of Political Science* 40 (3):587–611.

2012. "The Institutional Foundations of Legislative Speech." *American Journal of Political Science* 56 (3):520–37.

2015. *The Politics of Parliamentary Debate: Parties, Rebels and Representation*. Cambridge, United Kingdom: Cambridge University Press.

Rhodes, Martin. 2000. "Desperately Seeking a Solution: Social Democracy, Thatcherism and the 'Third Way' in British Welfare." *West European Politics* 23 (2):161–86.

Rice, Stuart A. 1925. "The Behavior of Legislative Groups: A Method of Measurement." *Political Science Quarterly* 40 (1). JSTOR:60–72.

Roberts, Jason M. 2005. "Minority Rights and Majority Power: Conditional Party Government and the Motion to Recommit in the House." *Legislative Studies Quarterly* 30 (2). Wiley Online Library:219–34.

Rogowski, Jon C. 2017. "Electoral Institutions and Legislative Particularism." *Legislative Studies Quarterly* 42:355–85.

Rohde, David W. 1991. *Parties and Leaders in the Postreform House*. Chicago, IL: University of Chicago Press.

Romer, Thomas, and Howard Rosenthal. 1978. "Political Resource Allocation, Controlled Agendas, and the Status Quo." *Public Choice* 33 (1):27–43.

Rosenthal, Howard. 1992. "The Unidimensional Congress Is Not the Result of Selective Gatekeeping." *American Journal of Political Science 36*(1): 31–35.

Schaufele, Brandon. 2014. "Dissent in Parliament as Reputation Building." *Available at SSRN* 2317466.

Schonhardt-Bailey, Cheryl. 2003. "Ideology, Party and Interests in the British Parliament of 1841–47." *British Journal of Political Science* 33 (04). Cambridge University Press:581–605.

Shepsle, Kenneth A. 1978. *The Giant Jigsaw Puzzle*. Chicago: University of Chicago Press.

Shepsle, Kenneth A., and Barry Weingast. 1987. "The Institutional Foundations of Committee Power." *The American Political Science Review* 81 (1):85–104.

Sieberer, Ulrich. 2006. "Party Unity in Parliamentary Democracies: A Comparative Analysis." *The Journal of Legislative Studies* 12 (2):150–78.

Slapin, Jonathan B., Justin H. Kirkland, Joseph A. Lazzaro, Patrick A. Leslie, and Tom O'Grady. 2018. "Ideology, Grandstanding and Strategic Party Disloyalty in the British Parliament." *The American Political Science Review* 112 (1):15–30.

Slapin, Jonathan B., and Sven-Oliver Proksch. 2008. "A Scaling Model for Estimating Time Series Party Positions from Texts." *American Journal of Political Science* 52 (3):705–22.

Slater, Dan, and Daniel Ziblatt. 2013. "The Enduring Indispensability of the Controlled Comparison." *Comparative Political Studies* 46 (10):1301–27.

Snyder Jr, James M. 1991. "On Buying Legislatures." *Economics & Politics 3* (2): 93–109.

Spirling, Arthur, and Iain McLean. 2006. "The Rights and Wrongs of Roll Calls." *Government and Opposition* 41 (4):581–88.

Spirling, Arthur, and Kevin Quinn. 2010. "Identifying Intraparty Voting Blocs in the UK House of Commons." *Journal of the American Statistical Association* 105 (490). Taylor & Francis:447–57.

Tavits, Margit. 2009. "The Making of Mavericks Local Loyalties and Party Defection." *Comparative Political Studies* 42 (6). Sage Publications:793–815.

Theriault, Sean M. 2013. *The Gingrich Senators: The Roots of Partisan Warfare in Congress.* Oxford, United Kingdom: Oxford University Press.

Tocqueville, Alexis de. 1966. *Democracy in America.* George Lawrence (trans.) and J. P. Mayer (ed). Harper & Row.

Tsebelis, George. 1990. *Nested Games.* University of California Press.

    1995. "Decision Making in Political Systems: Veto Players in Presidentialism, Parliamentarism, Multicameralism and Multipartyism." *British Journal of Political Science* 25 (3):289–325.

    2002. *Veto Players: How Political Institutions Work.* Princeton, NJ: Princeton University Press/Russell Sage.

Vivyan, Nick, and Markus Wagner. 2012. "Do Voters Reward Rebellion? The Electoral Accountability of MPs in Britain." *European Journal of Political Research* 51 (2). Wiley Online Library:235–64.

    2015. "What Do Voters Want from Their Local MP?" *The Political Quarterly* 86 (1):33–40.

Weingast, Barry R. 1979. "A Rational Choice Perspective on Congressional Norms." *American Journal of Political Science* 23 (2). JSTOR:245–62.

    1994. "Reflections on Distributive Politics and Universalism." *Political Research Quarterly 47* (2). JSTOR:319–27.

Wiseman, Alan E. 2004. "Tests of Vote-Buyer Theories of Coalition Formation in Legislatures." *Political Research Quarterly* 57 (3). Sage Publications: 441–50.

Wiseman, Alan E., and James R. Wright. 2008. "The Legislative Median and Partisan Policy." *Journal of Theoretical Politics 20*(1): 5–29.

Acknowledgments

We would like to thank the many people who have assisted with, coauthored, commented on, or labored through our development of this work. We are particularly thankful to Frances Lee, who has been an exceptional editor and supporter throughout this process, and to our two anonymous reviewers, both of whom carefully read the manuscript and provided us with valuable feedback. We are deeply indebted to the coauthors of our article, "Ideology, Grandstanding, and Strategic Party Disloyalty in the British Parliament," recently published (2018) in *American Political Science Review* – Tom O'Grady, Patrick Leslie, and Joseph Lazzaro. Much of our work on the House of Commons is based on research done for that article, and our coauthors were invaluable in its completion. Some of the theory and portions of the empirical analysis of Congress are revised versions of research originally published in our 2017 *Electoral Studies* article, "Ideology and Strategic Party Disloyalty in the US House of Representatives." We thank the publishers of these two articles for allowing us to reprint revised versions of that work here, enabling us to complete an argument that we could never have made in article format.

We have also received valuable support from our institutions: the University of Essex Department of Government, the University of Virginia Department of Politics, and especially the University of Houston Department of Political Science. Our current institutions have been wonderfully supportive of both of us, but none of this work would ever have been started without the steadfast support of our colleagues during our time together at the University of Houston. Finally, we would like to thank our partners and families. Our work often proves to be an inconvenience to our partners, but Aurelija and Laura have been exceptionally patient and supportive every step of the way.

Cambridge Elements ≡

American Politics

Frances E. Lee
University of Maryland-College Park
Frances E. Lee is Professor of Government and Politics at the University of Maryland-College Park. She is author of *Insecure Majorities: Congress and the Perpetual Campaign* (2016), *Beyond Ideology: Politics, Principles and Partisanship in the U.S. Senate* (2009), and coauthor of *Sizing Up the Senate: The Unequal Consequences of Equal Representation* (1999).

Advisory Board

About the Series
American Politics publishes authoritative contributions on American politics. Emphasizing works that address big, topical questions within the American political landscape, the series is open to all branches of the subfield and actively welcomes works that bridge subject domains. It publishes both original new research on topics likely to be of interest to a broad audience and state-of-the-art synthesis and reconsideration pieces that address salient questions and incorporate new data and cases to inform arguments.

Cambridge Elements ☰

American Politics

Elements in the Series

Policy Success in an Age of Gridlock: How the Toxic Substances Control Act was Finally Reformed
Lawrence S. Rothenberg
9781108628044

Roll Call Rebels: Strategic Dissent in the United States and United Kingdom
Justin H. Kirkland, Jonathan B. Slapin
9781108701556

A full series listing is available at: www.cambridge.org/core/series/elements-in-american-politics

Printed in the United States
By Bookmasters